Religion and Life

FIFTH EDITION

Victor W. Watton

Religion and Life

FIFTH EDITION

DYNAMIC LEARNING

Innovate • Motivate • Personalise

HODDER
EDUCATION
AN HACHETTE UK COMPANY

This material has been endorsed by Edexcel and offers high quality support for the delivery of Edexcel qualifications.

Edexcel endorsement does not mean that this material is essential to achieve any Edexcel qualification, nor does it mean that this is the only suitable material available to support any Edexcel qualification. No endorsed material will be used verbatim in setting any Edexcel examination and any resource lists produced by Edexcel shall include this and other appropriate texts. While this material has been through an Edexcel quality assurance process, all responsibility for the content remains with the publisher. Copies of official specifications for all Edexcel qualifications may be found on the Edexcel website – www.edexcel.org.uk

For photo credits and acknowledgments, please see page 144.

Hachette UK's policy is to use papers that are natural, renewable and recyclable products and made from wood grown in sustainable forests. The logging and manufacturing processes are expected to conform to the environmental regulations of the country of origin.

Orders: please contact Bookpoint Ltd, 130 Milton Park, Abingdon, Oxon OX14 4SB. Telephone: (44) 01235 827720. Fax: (44) 01235 400454. Lines are open 9.00–5.00, Monday to Saturday, with a 24-hour message answering service. Visit our website at www.hoddereducation.co.uk

© Victor W. Watton 2009
First published in 1996 by
Hodder Education,
An Hachette UK Company
338 Euston Road
London NW1 3BH

Second edition published (1999)
Third edition published (2001)
Fourth edition published (2005)
This fifth edition published (2009)

Impression number   5 4 3 2
Year   2013 2012 2011 2010 2009

Cover photos *l–r:* © Royal Observatory, Edinburgh/AATB/Science Photo Library; © Reuters/Corbis; © Digital Art/Corbis.
Illustrations by Ian Foulis, Daedalus and Barking Dog
Typeset in Electra LH Regular 12pt by Ian Foulis
Printed in Italy

A catalogue record for this title is available from the British Library.

ISBN: 978 0340 975 473

Religion and Life Teacher's Resource Book Pack, Fifth edition: 978 0340 975 503
Religion and Life Dynamic Learning Network CD-ROM, Second edition: 978 0340 986 806
Religion and Life Foundation Edition, Fifth edition: 978 0340 975 480
Religion and Life Revision Guide, Third edition: 978 0340 975 558

Contents

Section 3 **Marriage and the family**

Section 4 **Religion and community cohesion**

Introduction

This book covers all aspects of the Edexcel GCSE Religious Studies Unit 1: Religion and Life based on the study of Christianity and at least one other religion. This GCSE aims to get you to think about yourself, the society in which you live and the meaning of life.

- Each section of the book is a section of the GCSE specification, and the topics cover every part of that section. The main body of the text gives you all the information you need for each topic. The sources in the margin give you extra information for greater understanding of the topic.
- In the examination, you will have to answer one question on Section 1, one question on Section 2, one question on Section 3 and one question on Section 4.
- Wherever the symbol **C** occurs at the top of the page, it means that the topic also covers Key Stage 4 Citizenship. Your lesson might therefore also be a citizenship lesson.
- The word God is used throughout the religions so that you understand that names such as Allah and the Almighty are referring to the same God. Where dates are given, CE (Common Era) and BCE (Before the Common Era) are used to remove connections to one particular religion.

How to use the book

- Work through each topic. Words that you might not understand are in bold type so that you can look up their meanings in the relevant glossary at the end of the book (there is a glossary for general words, one for Christian words, one for Muslim words, one for Jewish words, one for Hindu words and one for Sikh words).
- Answer the questions at the end of the topic. For each topic there are examples of b, c and d questions and an exam tip on how to answer one of them. The exam tip gives you hints as to the approach that will gain you full marks. At the end of each section are examples and comments on all types of questions, a–d.
- You should study all the topics in section 1, but in sections 2, 3 and 4, *for the topics that cover Islam, Judaism, Hinduism and Sikhism, you only need to study one of these religions.*

I hope you enjoy your study of Religion and Life. Remember, Religious Studies is not about making you religious, it is about enabling you to think for yourself about religious and moral issues.

Section 1 Believing in God

Introduction

This section of the examination specification requires you to look at the issues surrounding belief in God based on the study of one religion. This book only studies Christianity in this section, but you could use another religion in your examination answers instead if you know about it in depth.

Reasons why people believe in God
You will need to understand the effects of, and give reasons for your own opinion about:
- a religious upbringing
- religious experience
- the design argument
- the argument from causation.

Reasons why some people do not believe in God
You will need to understand the effects of, and give reasons for your own opinion about:
- scientific explanations of the origins of the world
- unanswered prayers
- evil and suffering.

How Christians respond to the problems
You will need to understand the effects of, and give reasons for your own opinion about how Christians respond to:
- scientific explanations of the world
- unanswered prayers
- the problems of evil and suffering.

The media and belief in God
You will need to understand the effects of, and give reasons for your own opinion about how a television or radio programme about religion could affect attitudes to belief in God.

Topic 1.1 Religious upbringing

There are many reasons for believing in God. Some people are led to believe in God by one reason only, others find that a number of reasons taken together make it difficult not to believe in God. When people who already believe in God come across other reasons for believing in God, they find that this supports their belief in God.

You only need to know about a religious upbringing in one religion. This topic looks at a Christian religious upbringing, but if you know about another religion in depth you could use that instead.

The main features of a Christian upbringing

- Christian parents are likely to have their babies baptised. As part of this **sacrament**, the parents will promise to bring up their children as Christians and so encourage them to believe in God.
- Christian parents will teach their children to pray to God.
- Christian parents will take their children to worship God in church.
- Christian parents will send their children to Sunday School to learn about God and the Christian faith.
- Christian parents may send their children to a church school where they will be taught the National Curriculum in a Christian environment.
- As part of fulfilling their vows at **baptism**, Christian parents are likely to encourage their children to be confirmed as full members of the Church. The sacrament of **confirmation** involves lessons from the priest/**minister** about Christianity and the nature of God.
- This sacrament may involve a **religious experience** in the ceremony itself as the young person feels the presence of God through the prayers, vows and laying on of hands.

> **Minister:** *You have brought this child to be baptised, and you will receive her/him again to be trained in the doctrines, privileges and duties of the Christian religion. I ask you therefore:*
>
> *Will you provide for this your child a Christian home of love and faithfulness?*
>
> **Parents:** *With God's help, we will.*
>
> **From the Baptismal Service of the Methodist Church**

> *Holy baptism is the basis of the whole Christian life, the gateway to life in the Spirit ... and the door to which gives access to the other sacraments. Through baptism we are freed from sin and reborn as sons of God; we become members of Christ, are incorporated into the Church and made sharers in her mission: Baptism is the sacrament of regeneration through water and the word.*
>
> **Catechism of the Catholic Church 1213**

Why might being confirmed lead to, or support, belief in God?

How a religious upbringing may lead to, or support, belief in God

If you have had a Christian religious upbringing, belief in God will appear natural to you because:

- Your parents will have told you about God as part of their promises to bring you up as a Christian and young children believe what their parents tell them.
- Christians usually teach their children to pray to God. This will make the children believe that God exists because he listens to their prayers. If God did not exist, they and their parents would not waste their time praying to nothing. So because they've been brought up to pray, they believe that God must exist.
- Going to church and seeing so many people praying to God and worshipping God is likely to make them think that God must exist.
- Going to Sunday School would support belief in God because children would learn why Christians believe in God and what they believe about him.
- Going to a church school would have a similar effect, as God and Christianity would be a normal feature of school life. They will have RE lessons which teach them that God exists and the children are likely to believe it because their teachers tell them it is true.
- Being confirmed would be likely to support your belief, as you learn more about God in the confirmation lessons, and possibly have a religious experience when the bishop lays his hands on you.

I am a Catholic Christian because I was born to Catholic parents, and I was educated in a Catholic school. All my upbringing made me believe in God, and I have never really thought that God might not exist. God is a part of my life just as my parents and friends are.

A Catholic adult

Exam focus

'Explain' questions (part b) are where your Quality of Written Communication is tested, so you should answer these questions in a formal style of English, be careful with your spelling and try to use some specialist vocabulary (in this section baptism, sacrament, prayer, worship, confirmation, bishop would all be specialist vocabulary).

Questions

b Do you think children should follow the same religion as their parents? Give two reasons for your point of view. **4**

c Explain how a religious upbringing can lead to, or support, belief in God. **8**

d 'A religious upbringing forces children to believe in God.'
  i Do you agree? Give reasons for your opinion. **3**
  ii Give reasons why some people may disagree with you. **3**

Exam Tip

c 'Explain' means give reasons. To answer this question you should name four features of a religious upbringing and explain, in two or three sentences for each, how they might lead to belief in God. Remember your Quality of Written Communication will be assessed in your answer, so:
  - be careful with your spelling
  - use sentences and paragraphs
  - do not use bullet points
  - use specialist vocabulary.

SUMMARY

Having a religious upbringing is likely to lead to belief in God because children are taught that God exists and they spend most of their time with people who believe that God exists.

Topic 1.2 Religious experience

KEY WORDS

Conversion – when your life is changed by giving yourself to God.

Miracle – something which seems to break a law of science and makes you think only God could have done it.

Numinous – the feeling of the presence of something greater than you.

Prayer – an attempt to contact God, usually through words.

Religious experience is an event that people feel gives them direct contact with God. You need to know four types of religious experience: **numinous**, **conversion**, **miracle** and **prayer**.

1. The numinous

This is a feeling of the presence of God. When people are in a religious building, in a beautiful place or looking up at the stars on a clear night, they may be filled with the awareness that there is something greater than them, which they feel to be God. It is often described as an experience of the transcendent (something going beyond human experience and existing outside the material world). If someone has a numinous experience, it may lead them to believe in God because the experience will make them feel that God is real. If you become aware of a presence greater than you, you are likely to believe that that presence is God and so you will believe in him.

Example of the numinous

Father Yves Dubois has had numinous experiences while praying before a statue of Our Lady.

'Twice I have experienced the certainty of the presence of the Mother of God, which was an awareness of purity, holiness and love unlike anything I have ever known. Her holiness would have been frightening, but for the strong feeling of love and compassion.'
Source: Quoted in Christians in Britain Today, Hodder, 1991

Do you think Father Yves Dubois could doubt the existence of God after these numinous experiences?

2. Conversion and belief in God

This is the word used to describe an experience of God, which is so great that the person experiencing it wants to change their life and commit themselves to God in a special way. It can also be used to describe an experience, which causes someone to change their religion or change from **agnosticism** or **atheism** to belief in God. It is sometimes called a regenerative experience because it gives a feeling of being '**born again**'.

'I don't try to imagine a personal God; it suffices to stand in awe at the structure of the world, insofar as it allows our inadequate senses to appreciate it.'
Albert Einstein

If someone has a conversion experience, that will lead them to believe in God because they will feel that God is calling them to do something for him. When **St Paul** was on the road to Damascus and Jesus spoke to him from a bright light in the sky, telling him to become a Christian, he had little choice but to believe in God.

Example of a conversion

During the Civil War in the Lebanon, Raymond Nader was a commander in the Christian militia who led the fighting against Muslim militias. On a cold November night in 1994, he went to pray at the shrine of St Charbel. Suddenly the night got warmer and he felt surrounded by a great light. He reached out to touch the light and his arm was burned by what he, and the Church authorities, believed was the presence of St Charbel. The vision made him give up his work in the militia to work for Tele Lumiere, the only Christian television station in the Middle East. Tele Lumiere and Nader are dedicated to spiritual peace, the defence of human rights and dignity as a way of challenging the violence and horror of the Middle East.

Do you think that Raymond Nader would have been able to be an atheist after this conversion experience?

Saul was a persecutor of Christians and was on his way to Damascus to arrest the Christians there, when he had a vision of Jesus which blinded him. After this conversion experience, his sight recovered and he became a great Christian missionary and changed his name to Paul. This painting shows St Paul on the Road to Damascus. It was painted by Augustin Cranagh in 1560.

3. Miracles and belief in God

A miracle is an event that seems to break a law of science and the only explanation for which seems to be God. Miracles are recorded in most religions.

Example of a miracle

This statue of the Hindu God Ganesh appeared to drink milk from a spoon.

In September 1995, in a temple on the outskirts of Delhi, milk offered to a statue of the Hindu god Ganesh seemed to disappear into thin air. As news spread around the world, other Hindus tried this and found the same thing happening. The worshippers offered the god milk on a spoon and at least half the spoonful of milk disappeared. This happened at Hindu temples in Neasden, Wimbledon, Southall (all in London), Manchester and Leicester. The effect of the miracle was summarised by the chairman of the Southall Temple, Mr Bharbari, 'We believe this miracle, and those happening at other Hindu temples, may be a sign that a great Soul has descended, like Lord **Krishna** or Jesus Christ.'

Miracles can lead to belief in God because, if a miracle has really happened, it means that God has acted on the earth. If an atheist or agnostic witnesses a miracle, their first reaction will be to look for a natural explanation, as with the journalists who witnessed Ganesh drinking milk. However, if they cannot find one, it might lead them to believe in God. If you experience an event that seems to break all the laws of science, you will start searching for explanations and if the only explanation you can think of for what has happened is a miracle then you are likely to start believing in God. If a miracle really happens, then the people witnessing the miracle have had direct contact with God.

Thousands of letters sent each year to God end up in a sorting office in Jerusalem, it emerged this week. According to Associated Press, the letters arrive from all over the world in the city's undeliverable mail department. 'We have hundreds of thousands of letters sent to either God or Jesus Christ, and for some reason they all end up in Jerusalem,' said a post office spokesman, Yitzhak Rabihya. In one letter an Israeli man asked God for 5,000 shekels to ease his poverty. Postal workers were so moved that they sent him 4,300 shekels. 'After a month the same man wrote again to God,' Mr Rabiya explained, 'but this time he wrote, "Oh, thank you God for the contribution, but next time please don't send it through those postmen. They're thieves, they stole 700 shekels."'

The Times, 4 October 2003

4. Prayer

All religious believers think that they can make contact with God through prayer. These prayers may be formal prayers offered in worship such as the Christian prayers in the **Eucharist** (communion service), the Muslim prayers offered in **Salah** or the Hindu prayers offered in the **arti** ceremony. They may also be very informal where a believer makes their own prayer to God in their own private place.

If the person praying feels that God is listening to the prayer, then they are likely to believe that God exists. Perhaps the biggest reason anyone can have for believing in God is when their private prayer is answered, for example when someone prays for a sick loved one to recover and they do. Atheists and agnostics do not usually pray, but if they did, because someone they loved had an incurable illness and it seemed worth a try, if the prayer was answered, it may well lead them to believe in God.

George W. Bush's religious experiences led him to believe in God and change his life.

Example of prayer leading to belief

About ten years later, I began to pray for my children's safety, and this became a habit which I have never lost, and often the answer to such prayer is spectacular. I find it best to live as if the soul of man were in communion with a superhuman force which makes for righteousness. May I add that since this belief grew in me, I feel that I had grown, as if my mind had stretched to take in the vast universe and be part of it.

Source: Alister Hardy Trust, Oxford

Any religious believer who has any form of religious experience will find that the experience supports their belief in God and makes it stronger because they now have more direct evidence for God's existence.

Questions

b Do you think miracles prove that God exists? Give two
   reasons for your point of view.   **4**
c Explain how religious experience can lead to, or support,
   belief in God.   **8**
d 'Religious experiences prove that God exists.'
   i Do you agree? Give reasons for your opinion.   **3**
   ii Give reasons why some people may disagree with you.   **3**

Exam Tip

b You should already have thought about this, and you just have to give two reasons for your opinion. For example, if you think miracles prove God's existence, you could use these two reasons:
   ● if a miracle happens there is no explanation for it except that God caused it to happen
   ● Christians believe that Jesus rising from the dead proves he was God's Son because only God could rise from the dead.

Exam focus

You must decide what you think about the issues and ideas you study. For this topic you should have thought about whether there is such a thing as the numinous and whether it means God exists; you should have thought about whether conversions really happen and whether they prove God exists; whether you believe in miracles and whether a miracle would prove that God exists; whether prayer is valuable. The questions are meant to be quite easy and to get full marks you just need to give two reasons.

SUMMARY

People claim to experience God in miracles, answered prayers, the numinous and conversion. Religious experience makes people feel that God is real.

Topic 1.3 The argument from design and belief in God

Could this car have been made without the design?

What is design?

Any complex mechanism is designed for a purpose. Design involves things working together according to a plan to produce something that was intended. If you look at a car you can see that the fuel powers an engine which turns a shaft which turns the wheels and so makes a self-propelled vehicle to allow people to travel further and more easily. A look at any part of the car makes you think that the car has been designed.

Evidence of design in the world

Laws of science

A main reason why some people think the universe has been designed is because the universe works according to laws. The laws of gravity, electricity, magnetism, motion, bonding, gases, etc., all involve complex things working together.

DNA

DNA seems to be another piece of evidence of design in the world. DNA is a nucleic acid which forms the material of all living organisms.

- DNA is made up of two strands that form a ladder-like structure, which forms a right-hand spiral called a double helix.
- The DNA molecule replicates by unzipping and using each strand as a template to form a new strand.
- These new DNA strands are then passed on to daughter cells during cell division.

The structure of DNA and its formation of templates seem to indicate a design or blueprint for the structure of organisms.

Evolution

Some scientists also see evidence of design in the process of evolution where complex life forms develop from simple ones.

Beauty of nature

Artists see evidence of design in the beauties of nature where sunsets, mountains and oceans appear to have beauty which an artist would have to spend a long time designing.

Science, design and God

The question about the origins of the world and of man has been the object of many scientific studies that have splendidly enriched our knowledge of the age and dimensions of the cosmos, the development of life-forms and the appearance of man. These discoveries invite us to even greater admiration for the greatness of the Creator.

Catechism of the Catholic Church

Paley's Watch

If you came across a watch in an uninhabited place, you could not say it had been put there by chance. The complexity of its mechanism would make you say it had a designer. The universe is a far more complex mechanism than a watch, and so, if a watch needs a watchmaker, the universe needs a universe maker. As the only being that could design the universe would be God, it follows that God must exist.

Paley's Watch Argument for the Existence of God

How the appearance of design may lead to, or support, belief in God

Using the appearance of design to lead to belief in God is often called the argument from design (the most famous version is Paley's Watch). It goes like this:

- Anything that has been designed needs a designer.
- There is plenty of evidence that the world has been designed (laws of science, DNA, evolution, beauties of nature).
- If the world has been designed, the world must have a designer.
- The only possible designer of something as beautiful and complex as the world would be God.
- Therefore the appearance of design in the world proves that God exists.

This argument shows how the appearance of design in the world can lead people who are not sure about God to believe that he exists; and how it will give extra reasons for believing in God to those who already believe.

How the appearance of design may not lead to belief in God

Many people think the argument from design does not lead to belief in God because:

- The argument ignores the evidence of lack of design in the universe, for example volcanoes, earthquakes, hurricanes, diseases.
- All the evidence for design can be explained by science without needing even to think of God.
- The argument does not refer to the existence of dinosaurs which must have been a part of design, but no one thinks they could have been part of a design plan for the world.
- The argument only proves that the universe has a designer, not God. The designer could be many gods, an evil God, a God who used this universe as a trial run so that he could create a better one.

Exam focus

Evaluation questions
- Decide what you think about the statement.
- Give at least three brief reasons, or two longer reasons, or a paragraph reason, supporting your point of view.
- Look at the opposite point of view and give at least three brief reasons, or two longer reasons, or a paragraph reason, for why people have this view.

The evaluation questions mean that you must always be aware not only of your own point of view about a topic, but also about the opposite point of view.

REMEMBER
One of your points of view should always be a religious one.

SUMMARY

The universe seems to be designed. Anything that is designed must have a designer. Therefore God must exist because only God could have designed the Universe.

Questions

b Do you think God designed the world? Give two reasons for your point of view. **4**
c Explain why the design argument leads some people to believe in God. **8**
d 'The design argument proves that God exists.'
  i Do you agree? Give reasons for your opinion. **3**
  ii Give reasons why some people may disagree with you. **3**

Exam tip

d Use the evaluation technique from this page.
  - Arguments for design would be the design argument itself.
  - Arguments against would come from why some people disagree with the argument from design.

Topic 1.4 The argument from causation and belief in God

What is causation?

This is the process whereby one thing causes another. It is often known as cause and effect; in the example below, the cause would be pressing the brake pedal and the effect would be the car slowing down.

Evidence of causation in the world

Cause and effect seem to be a basic feature of the world. Whatever we do has an effect. If I do my homework, I will please my parents and/or teachers. If I do not do my homework, I will annoy my parents and/or teachers. Modern science has developed through looking at causes and effects and in particular looking for single causes of an effect. Just as my parents' happiness may be caused by other things than my doing my homework, so the increase in someone's heart rate may be caused by other things than exercise. So when a scientist tries to discover the cause of increase in heart rate, he/she tries to reduce all the variables (for example arrival of girl/boyfriend) so that a single cause can be identified. Science seems to show that, when investigated sufficiently, any effect has a cause and any cause has an effect.

The argument from causation

The appearance of causation in the world is often called the First Cause Argument and goes like this:

> If we look at things in the world, we see that they have a cause; for example, ice is caused by the temperature falling and water becoming solid at below 0°C.

> Anything caused to exist must be caused to exist by something else because to cause your own existence, you would have to exist before you exist, which is nonsense.

> You cannot keep going back with causes because in any causal chain you have to have a beginning; for example, you have to have water to produce ice.
> So if the universe has no First Cause, then there would be no universe, but as there is a universe, there must be a First Cause.

> The only possible First Cause of the universe is God, therefore God must exist.

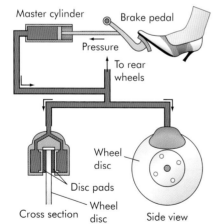

For example, putting your foot on the brake when driving a car causes hydraulic pressure in the brake pipes, which causes the brake pads to put pressure on the discs, which causes the wheels to stop turning, which causes the car to slow down.

This argument makes people think that the universe, the world and humans must have come from somewhere, they must have had a cause. As God is the only logical cause of the universe, it makes them think that God must exist, or it supports their belief in God if they already believe.

People who believe that causation proves that God exists often use the example of a goods train. Each wagon is caused to move by the wagon that is pulling it. But although each wagon is caused to move by another wagon, which is caused to move by another wagon, etc., the whole process can only be explained if there is an engine that is not moved by something in front but is 'an unmoved mover'. In the same way, the process seen in the world – of things being caused or moved by something else – can only be explained if there is an Unmoved Mover causing it all to happen and this could only be God.

Why some people disagree with the argument

Some people may think the argument from causation does not prove that God exists because:

- Why should the causes stop at God? If everything needs a cause then God must need a cause.
- A better explanation is that the matter of the Universe itself is eternal and so the process of causes goes on for ever.
- Even if the First Cause were to exist it would not have to be God, it could be any sort of creator.

Does the universe need a First Cause? If so, and that First Cause is God, does God need a cause?

> *Behold! In the creation of the heavens and the earth; in the alternation of the Night and the Day ... Here indeed are signs for a people that are wise.*
>
> **Surah 2:164**

People who believe in the First Cause often use the example of a line of railway wagons, claiming that just as the wagons need an engine to explain how they are moving, so the universe needs God to explain how it is working.

Questions

b Do you think God is the cause of the universe? Give two reasons for your point of view. **4**

c Explain how the argument from causation may lead to belief in God. **8**

d 'The argument from causation proves that God exists.'
  i Do you agree? Give reasons for your opinion. **3**
  ii Give reasons why some people may disagree with you. **3**

Exam Tip

c To answer this question, you need to outline the argument and make sure you emphasise the conclusion (the last step in the flowchart and the first paragraph after the flowchart) so that you show exactly how it might lead to belief in God. For tips on Quality of Written Communication, look at page 3.

SUMMARY

The way everything seems to have a cause makes people think the universe must have a cause, and the only possible cause of the universe is God, so God must exist.

Topic 1.5 Scientific explanations of the world and agnosticism and atheism

KEY WORDS

Agnosticism – not being sure whether God exists.

Atheism – believing that God does not exist.

An alternative to the Big Bang?

Scientists from Princeton University claim that the universe began not with a Big Bang but a collision with another universe. According to the scientists, a weak attraction brought two universes together, creating a collision that made particles and energy. The scientists claim that the theory explains many observations of the universe better than the Big Bang. Recent observations of background radiation from the 'edges' of the cosmos, relics of early moments of the universe, reveal a startling homogeneity in all directions. The Big Collision would have created almost instantaneously the energy and matter in all regions of the newly blossoming universe. This explains the consistency or smoothness of the universe. The new model allows for the slight ripples in the cosmic fabric that created the seeds for the formation of galaxies and large-scale structure in the universe, the researchers said.

Science Journal, April 2002

Science explains how the world came into being in this way:

- Matter is eternal, it can neither be created nor destroyed, only changed (scientists call this the law of thermo-dynamics).
- About 15 billion years ago, the matter of the universe became so compressed that it produced a huge explosion (the Big Bang).
- As the matter of the universe flew away from the explosion, the forces of gravity and other laws of science joined some of the matter into stars and, about 5 billion years ago, the solar system was formed.
- The combination of gases on the earth's surface produced primitive life forms, like amoeba.
- The genetic structure of these life forms produces changes (mutations).
- Any change that is better suited to living in the environment will survive and reproduce.
- Over millions of years new life forms were produced leading to vegetation, then invertebrate animals, then vertebrates and finally, about 2.5 million years ago, humans evolved.

Evidence for the Big Bang

The main evidence for the Big Bang theory is called the Red Shift Effect (shown below) where the red shift in light from other galaxies is evidence that the universe is expanding.

Evidence for evolution

The evidence for the theory of evolution is the fossil record (the evidence from fossils of life developing from simple to complex), and the similarities between life forms being discovered through genetic research (about 50 per cent of human DNA is the same as that of a cabbage).

How the scientific explanation of the world may lead to agnosticism or atheism

Science can explain where the world came from and where humans came from without any reference to God.

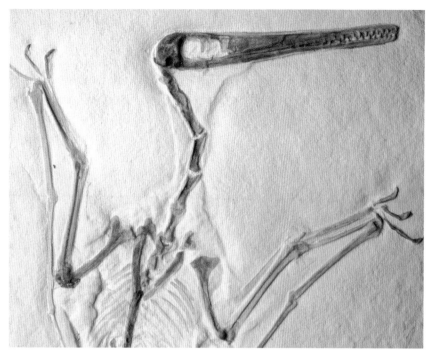

This Pterodactylus dinosaur fossil is from the Late Jurassic era (over 145.5 million years ago).

This may lead some people to be **agnostic**, that is they are unsure whether there is a God or not. The argument that you need God to explain why we are here is no longer valid for them.

Other people may be led to become **atheists** and be sure there is no God because they believe that, if God exists, he must have made the world and he must be the only explanation of the world. The scientific explanation of the world and humans without any reference to God is proof to such people that God does not exist.

Questions

b Do you agree with the scientific explanation of the world? Give two reasons for your point of view. **4**

c Explain why the scientific explanation of the world leads some people to become atheists or agnostics. **8**

d 'Science proves that God did not create the universe.'

  i Do you agree? Give reasons for your opinion. **3**

  ii Give reasons why some people may disagree with you. **3**

Exam Tip

d Use the answering evaluation questions advice from page 9. The arguments for the statement are in this topic, the arguments against are in Topic 1.6.

SUMMARY

Science says that matter is eternal and that the universe began when this matter exploded. The solar system came out of the explosion, and the nature of the earth allowed life to develop through evolution.

Topic 1.6 How one religion responds to scientific explanations of the world

Has all animal life come from the animals saved on Noah's ark?

There are three Christian responses to scientific explanations of the world.

Response One

Many Christians believe that the scientific explanations are true. However, they believe that the scientific explanation does not mean that everyone should be agnostic or atheist. They believe that the scientific explanation proves that God created the universe because of such reasons as:

- The Big Bang had to be at exactly the right micro second. If it had been too soon it would have been too small to form stars; if it had been too late, everything would have flown away too fast for stars to form.
- There had to be scientific laws such as gravity for the matter of the universe to form solar systems, and only God could have made the laws on which the universe is based.
- Life on earth requires carbon to be able to bond with four other atoms and water molecules. This could not have happened by chance, so God must have ensured it happened.

Response Two

Some Christians believe that science is wrong and the Bible is right. They claim that all the evidence there is of the Big Bang and evolution can be explained by the effects of Noah's flood (which must have totally changed rock formations) and the Apparent Age theory.

Apparent Age theory claims that if you accept the Bible view, then when Adam was made the earth was six days old, but to Adam it would have looked billions of years old because trees would have been created with rings showing them hundreds of years old; the Grand Canyon would have looked 2 billion years old when it was one second old.

Therefore they believe that God created the universe in the way described in the Bible – this response is often called **creationism**.

> *What is revealed of the divine in the human life of Jesus is also to be discerned in the cosmic story of creation.*
>
> **J. Polkinghorne in *Science and Creation***

Response 3

Some Christians believe that both the scientific explanations and the Bible are correct. They claim that the main points of the Bible story fit with science. One of God's days could be millions or billions of years. They claim that Genesis 1:3 'God said, "Let there be light"', is a direct reference to the Big Bang and that the order in which God creates life as described in Genesis – plants, trees, fish, birds, animals, humans – is the same order as described in the theory of evolution for the development of species.

WAP WAP WAP

Can we know how God created the world?

> The point is that, for the existence of any forms of life that we may conceive, the necessary environment, whatever its nature, must be complex and dependent on a multiplicity of coincident conditions, such as are not reasonably attributable to blind forces or to pure mechanism.
>
> **F. R. Tennant in** *The Existence of God*

Questions

b Do you think science shows that God did not design the world? Give two reasons for your point of view. **4**

c Choose one religion and explain how its followers respond to scientific explanations of the world. **8**

d 'The universe could only have been made by God.'

   i Do you agree? Give reasons for your opinion. **3**

   ii Give reasons why some people may disagree with you. **3**

Exam tip

c You must choose a religion so begin with the words 'In Christianity'. 'Explaining how' means explaining the responses of Christianity to the scientific explanation. You should take two responses and explain them in some detail to reach level 4. For tips on Quality of Written Communication, look at page 3.

SUMMARY

- Many Christians accept the scientific explanations but believe they show that God created the Universe through the Big Bang.
- Some Christians say the scientific explanations are wrong and the biblical story of creation is fact because it is the word of God.
- Some Christians believe that both science and the Bible are true because one of God's days could be billions of years.

Topic 1.7 How unanswered prayers may lead to agnosticism or atheism

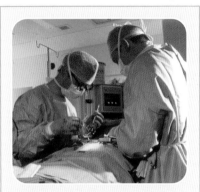

Prayer appears to have no effect on patients undergoing heart surgery, a new study has found. Researchers at Duke University Medical Center in North Carolina followed the progress of 750 patients, half of whom were prayed for by a team of Christians, Jews, Buddhists and Muslims. Those who were prayed for fared no better than those who were not.

The Times, 18 October 2003

If God exists, shouldn't those who pray have better results than those who do not?

As can be seen in Topic 1.2 Religious experience (pages 4–7), one reason for people believing in God is that when they pray, they feel the presence of God and/or their prayers seem to be answered by God. However, prayer can also lead people to become agnostics or atheists.

Not feeling God's presence when praying

Prayer can be defined as 'an attempt to contact God, usually through words'. So when people pray, they are attempting to contact God. Many religious people claim that when they pray, they feel that God is there listening to their prayers.

However, other people say their prayers in church and at home, but never feel the presence of God when they pray. This is likely to make them feel that something is wrong: either they are not praying correctly, or there is no God listening to them. They may ask for advice from people they respect within the religion and try even harder in their praying. But if, despite all their efforts, they still have no feeling of the presence of God when they pray, then they may begin to question whether God is there at all. In other words, the feeling that no one is listening to their prayers leads them to agnosticism, or even atheism.

Prayers not being answered

Even more likely to make people reject belief in God are unanswered prayers. Christians believe that God is their loving heavenly father who will answer their prayers. In some churches, they are likely to be told of people whose prayers have been answered by God. For example, many Catholic Christians believe that St Jude is the patron saint for those who have no other hope of help and many Catholics believe that St Jude has helped them after they prayed to him. This is one example from a Catholic Christian.

Example of an answered prayer

I spent five years with a boyfriend who would not commit himself to marriage. I was severely depressed and prayed to St Jude for help. With St Jude's intervention, my prayers were finally answered, and at last I am happily married.

Thank you St Jude, I promise to let your good deeds be known to all.

However, if another person prays, and their prayer is not answered, they may begin to wonder about a God who answers some people's prayers, but not others.

If parents have a child suffering from leukaemia, for example, and they pray to God for help, yet the child still dies, this may make them question or reject the existence of God. If there was a God who helped Jairus' daughter recover from a life-threatening disease, surely he would have helped their child recover. As their child did not recover, they may begin to think that God does not exist.

If prayers continue to be unanswered, especially if the person believes they are praying for good things like the end of wars, or the end of a terrible drought in a developing country, then the unanswered prayers become evidence that God does not exist. In this way, unanswered prayers can lead a person to become an agnostic or an atheist.

A young missionary couple asked the members of their church to pray that they would have a safe journey to their new posting in Nepal. However, the plane crashed killing them and their three young children.

Quoted in *If I were God I'd Say Sorry*

Why do you think the church's prayers were unanswered?

Questions

b Do you think unanswered prayers prove that God does not exist? Give two reasons for your point of view. **4**

c Explain why unanswered prayers may lead some people to become atheists. **8**

d 'God always answers prayers.'
   i Do you agree? Give reasons for your opinion. **3**
   ii Give reasons why some people may disagree with you. **3**

Exam Tip

d Use the evaluation technique on page 9. Evidence for God answering prayers is in Topic 1.8. Evidence against God answering prayers is in this topic.

SUMMARY

If people do not feel God's presence when they pray, or if people pray for good things, but their prayers are not answered, this might make some people doubt God's existence. If God does not answer prayers, how do you know he exists?

Topic 1.8 How one religion responds to unanswered prayers

Gracious Lord, oh bomb the Germans

Spare their women for Thy Sake,

And if that is not too easy

We will pardon Thy Mistake,

But, gracious Lord, whate'er shall be,

Don't let anyone bomb me.

In Westminster Abbey, John Betjeman

Why do you think God might not have answered this prayer supposedly made by an Englishwoman during the Second World War?

Most Christians believe that God answers all prayers and that what seem to be unanswered prayers can be explained in many different ways.

- If what you pray for is selfish, for example, 'Please God, help me to pass this exam', it would be wrong of God to allow you to pass the exam if you had not revised for it. So God is answering your prayer by encouraging you to work hard for what you want to achieve.
- If what you pray for is personal, for example, 'Please cure my Grandad from his cancer', your prayer may not be answered in the way you expect because God has different plans and may be wanting your Grandad to enter heaven.
- Human parents do not always give their children what they ask for, but they do give them what they need. In the same way God may be answering our prayer by giving us what we need rather than what we have asked for.
- Christians believe that God loves people and they trust God's love to do what is best for us. They believe that God's omnipotence and benevolence mean that he knows them better than they know themselves, therefore they trust God to answer their prayers in the best possible way, even though it does not look like a direct answer.
- Jesus said that his followers must have faith to have their prayers answered. Modern Christians have faith that God will answer all prayers in a way designed for the long-term good of the person praying, or the people prayed for, even though God's way might be a different way from the expected one.

Questions

b Do you think prayer is a waste of time? Give two reasons for your point of view. **4**

c Choose one religion and explain how its followers respond to unanswered prayers. **8**

d 'Unanswered prayers prove that God does not exist.'
   i Do you agree? Give reasons for your opinion. **3**
   ii Give reasons why some people may disagree with you. **3**

Exam tip

b You should already have thought about this, and you just have to give two reasons for your opinion. For example, if you think prayer is not a waste of time, you could use these two reasons:
- For people who believe in God, prayer is the best way to improve their relationship with God.
- If God answers your prayers, for example, by helping you pass an exam, you are not going to think prayer is waste of time.

SUMMARY

Christians believe that God cannot answer selfish prayers. But he answers all other prayers, though not always in the way people expect, because his answers have to fit in with his overall plans.

Topic 1.9 Evil and suffering

Evil and suffering can take two forms:

1. Moral evil

This is evil that is caused by humans misusing their **free will** (the human faculty of making choices). It is always possible to choose to do something good or something evil. Humans choosing to do evil makes a **moral evil**.

War is a good example of moral evil. Wars cause large amounts of suffering. Not only are military personnel on both sides made to suffer, but modern warfare also involves the use of weapons that kill and maim large numbers of innocent civilians. All wars are caused by the actions of humans who could have chosen to act differently. Suicide bombers actively choose to cause suffering to innocent people, who are likely to include babies and children, in order to draw attention to their cause.

Rape, murder and burglary are clear examples of moral evil. Less clear would be such suffering as famines where humans making wrong choices may have caused the suffering, for example, landowners growing cash crops like cotton instead of food in order to make more money. However, the famine could have been caused by something out of the control of humans, such as a lack of rain.

Christians often call acts of moral evil **sins** because they are against what God wants humans to do (as revealed to them, for example, in the **Ten Commandments**).

2. Natural evil

Natural evil is suffering that has not been caused by humans. Earthquakes, floods, volcanoes, drought, tsunamis, hurricanes, tornadoes, cancers and so on are not actually caused by humans, but they result in massive amounts of human suffering.

> ## KEY WORDS
>
> **Free will** – the idea that human beings are free to make their own choices.
>
> **Moral evil** – actions done by humans which cause suffering.
>
> **Natural evil** – things which cause suffering but have nothing to do with humans.

> *You shall not murder.*
> *You shall not commit adultery.*
> *You shall not steal.*
> *You shall not give false testimony ...*
> *You shall not covet ...*
>
> **The last five of the Ten Commandments, Exodus 20:13–17**
>
> **Would breaking these lead to moral evil?**

The aftermath of the tsunami of December 2004 in Southeast Asia. This event caused many people to ask how God could let something like that happen.

KEY WORDS

Omni-benevolent – the belief that God is all-good.

Omnipotent – the belief that God is all-powerful.

Omniscient – the belief that God knows everything that has happened and everything that is going to happen.

I cannot imagine any omnipotent sentient being sufficiently cruel to create the world we inhabit.

The Severed Head,
Iris Murdoch

How are atheists produced? In probably nine cases out of ten, what happens is something like this:

A beloved husband, or wife, or child, or sweetheart is gnawed to death by cancer, stultified by epilepsy, struck dumb and helpless by apoplexy, or strangled by diphtheria; and the looker-on, after praying vainly to God to refrain from such horrible and wanton cruelty, indignantly repudiates faith in the divine monster.

St Joan, George Bernard Shaw (1856–1950)

How evil and suffering cause people to question or reject belief in God

Some people cannot believe that a good God would have designed a world with natural evils in it. If they had been God, they would not have created a world with floods, earthquakes, volcanoes, cancers, etc.; and, as they believe God must be better than them, they cannot believe that God would have done so. They find it easier to believe that these features are a result of the earth evolving by accident from the Big Bang and so they question or reject God's existence.

Some people cannot believe in a God who allows humans to cause so much evil and suffering when he could stop it if he wanted to. If God exists, he must have known what Adolf Hitler would do, so why did he not give Hitler a heart attack before all the suffering caused by the Second World War and the Holocaust? As the suffering was not stopped, this may mean that God does not exist.

A mother crying after her home has been destroyed by an earthquake. Would a good omnipotent God cause so much suffering?

Philosophers express the problem in this way:
- If God is **omnipotent** (all-powerful), he must be able to remove evil and suffering from the world.
- If God is **omni-benevolent** (all-good), he must want to remove evil and suffering from the world because they cause so much unhappiness.
- It follows that, if God exists, there should be no evil or suffering in the world.
- As there is evil and suffering in the world, either God is not omnipotent, or God is not omni-benevolent, or God does not exist.

This is often connected with God's omniscience, because if God knows everything that is going to happen, he must have known all the evil and suffering that would come from creating the universe in the way he did. Therefore he should have created the universe in a different way to avoid evil and suffering.

Most religious believers (especially Christians, Jews and Muslims) believe that God is omnipotent, omni-benevolent and **omniscient**. So the existence of evil and suffering challenges their beliefs about God, and as these beliefs come from their holy books, it challenges the whole of their religion.

For many religious believers evil and suffering become a problem when they come into contact with it. So, if they experience the suffering caused by a natural disaster like an earthquake, or if their child dies from a disease, the problem can sometimes change them into an atheist or agnostic.

Should there be the sufferings of conjoined twins in a world created by an omnipotent and benevolent God?

Questions

b Do you think evil and suffering show that God does not exist? Give two reasons for your point of view. **4**

c Explain how the existence of evil and suffering may lead some people to deny God's existence. **8**

d 'A loving God would not let us suffer.'
  i Do you agree? Give reasons for your opinion. **3**
  ii Give reasons why some people may disagree with you. **3**

Exam Tip

c Look at the problems caused to people's lives by evil and suffering and explain why these may stop them believing in God – remember to include the philosophers' explanation. For tips on Quality of Written Communcation, look at page 3.

SUMMARY

Some people do not believe in God because they think that there would be no evil and suffering in a world created by a good and powerful God. A good God should not want such things to happen, and a powerful God ought to be able to get rid of them but does not.

Topic 1.10 How one religion responds to the problem of evil and suffering

There are several Christian responses to the problem of evil and suffering, and most Christians would combine at least two to explain why evil and suffering is compatible with God's omni-benevolence and omnipotence. However, almost all Christians would begin with response one.

Response One

Christians believe that God wants them to help those who suffer. The **New Testament** teaches Christians that Jesus regarded evil and suffering as something to be fought against. Jesus healed the sick, fed the hungry, challenged those who were evil and even raised the dead.

Christians feel that they should follow the example of Jesus and try to remove evil and suffering. Many Christians believe from the Bible that God must have a reason for allowing evil and suffering, but the reason is beyond human comprehension, so the correct response of Christians is to follow the example of Jesus and fight against evil and suffering.

Most Christians respond to the problem of evil and suffering by praying for those who suffer. This is called intercessionary prayer and all Christian services include prayers of intercession asking God to help those who suffer from poverty, sickness, famine, war, and so on. Christians believe that prayer is a powerful way of dealing with a problem.

Christians also respond by helping those who suffer. Many Christians become doctors, nurses and social workers, for example, so that they can help to reduce the amount of suffering in the world. Christians have also founded charities to help to remove suffering.

The Children's Society was founded by Christians to help children suffering from family breakdowns. Christian Aid and CAFOD were founded by Christians to help to remove the suffering caused by lack of development.

A CAFOD (Catholic Agency for Overseas Development) partner with armed child soldiers. Do you think Christian workers feel compelled to do this kind of work by the words of Jesus in Matthew 25?

Exam focus

A response is a way of answering the problem of evil and suffering. Exam questions are likely to use the words 'The response of one religion' or 'How do the followers of one religion respond to'. They mean the same thing.

Then the righteous will answer him, 'Lord, when did we see you hungry and feed you, or thirsty and give you something to drink? When did we see you a stranger and invite you in, or needing clothes and clothe you? When did we see you sick or in prison and go to visit you?' The King will reply, 'I tell you the truth, whatever you did for one of the least of these brothers of mine, you did for me.'

Matthew 25:37–40

Response Two

Many Christians respond by claiming that evil and suffering is not God's fault. They claim that, by making humans with free will, God created a world in which evil and suffering will come about through humans misusing their free will. So evil and suffering is a problem caused by humans, not God.

Response Three

Often connected with the free will response is the Christian belief that the evil and suffering involved in this life

'The Children's Society helped me get my life back after I ran away from home and started taking drugs – I don't know what I would have done without them.'

are not a problem because they are part of a plan in which those who suffer will be rewarded by eternal paradise after they die. Most Christians claim that this life is a preparation for paradise. If people are to improve their souls they need to face evil and suffering in order to become good, kind and loving. They claim that the evil and suffering of this life is something God cannot remove if he is going to give people the chance to become good people. But, in the end, he will show his omni-benevolence and omnipotence by rewarding them in heaven.

Response Four

Some Christians claim that God has a reason for not using his power to remove evil and suffering, but humans cannot understand it. God is divine and there is no way humans can understand the workings of the divine mind. Most Christians who respond in this way connect it with response one.

> While God cannot be said to be responsible for the world's evil, he has assumed responsibility for it by creating a world such as ours in the first place. That is to say, he is not a distant God, but somehow present in the evil, loving and suffering with those who suffer it, and enabling people to triumph over it by bringing good out of evil.
>
> *Private Notes*, Peter de Rosa, a twentieth-century Christian thinker

> God is in the cancer as he is in the sunset, and is to be met and responded to in each. Both are faces of God, the one terrible, the other beautiful. Neither as such is the face of love, but, as in the case of the cross for the Christian, even the worst can be transformed and vanquished. The problem of evil is not how God can will it, but its power to threaten meaningless and separation.
>
> *Exploration into God*, J. A. T. Robinson, a twentieth-century Christian thinker SCM 1967

Questions

b Do you think God allows us to suffer? Give two reasons for your point of view. **4**

c Choose one religion and explain how its followers respond to the problem of evil and suffering. **8**

d 'Evil and suffering in the world prove that God does not exist.'

   i Do you agree? Give reasons for your opinion. **3**

   ii Give reasons why some people may disagree with you. **3**

Exam Tip

d Use the evaluation technique on page 9. Evidence for evil and suffering proving God does not exist is in Topic 1.9. Evidence against evil and suffering proving God does not exist is in this topic.

SUMMARY

Christians respond to the problem of evil and suffering by:

- praying for those who suffer
- helping those who suffer
- claiming that evil and suffering are the fault of humans misusing their free will
- claiming that evil and suffering are part of a test to prepare people for heaven.

Topic 1.11 How two programmes about religion could affect a person's attitude to belief in God

You have to study two programmes about religion in depth and assess how they could affect a person's attitude to belief in God.

Why do you think *The Convent* reality show became so popular?

Where have we come from? Why are we here? How should we live? BBC Religion exists to ask the big questions that underlie all human life and explore the different ways in which people try to answer them, whether through worship, prayer, or simply giving food for thought.

The aim of Religious Broadcasting by the BBC

The programmes do not have to be factual programmes about religion (for example, a worship programme like *Songs of Praise*, a reality show like *The Convent*, or *A Seaside Parish*, a documentary like *The Miracles of Jesus*, or a discussion programme like *The Sunday Edition*). The crucial thing about the programmes is that they should be about belief in God, so programmes like *The Simpsons* and *The Vicar of Dibley* could be used as long as they have sufficient content about belief in God. Your programme does not have to be on television, it could be a radio programme or a film.

When you have chosen your two programmes, you need to make notes on the following for each of them:

1 Write a summary of the programme.

2 Decide which parts of the programme might have encouraged belief in God in some people and write down four reasons (using evidence from the programme) for this.

3 Decide which parts of the programme might have encouraged some people not to believe in God and write down four reasons (using evidence from the programme) for this.

4 Decide what effect the programme had on your own attitude to belief in God and write down four reasons for this.

Sample programme – *Songs of Praise*

On Sunday 3 February 2008, *Songs of Praise* came from St Wilfred's, Harrogate. Although the interviews at the Royal Pump Room Museum and at St Wilfred's Church might have had little effect on people's attitude to belief in God, two other interviews, and the hymns might have.

Mark Pallant, Head of Music at St Aidan's Church of England High School, talked about his own faith, and how he feels that music can put people in touch with God, the creator of the universe. If you had watched this programme, you would need to note the points Mark made and decide whether they would encourage you to believe in God. If not, you would need to write down reasons why they did not affect your beliefs. Then you would need to note down reasons why some people might disagree with you.

Phil Willis, the MP for Harrogate, talked about how he changed from an agnostic to a Christian through someone he used to teach with. You would need to note the points Phil made and decide whether they would encourage you to believe in God. If not, you would need to write down reasons why they did not affect your beliefs. Then you would need to note down reasons why some people might disagree with you.

You would need to watch the singing of the hymns, listen to the music and think about the words to gain evidence about whether or not they would influence attitudes to belief in God. Remember you need evidence for your point of view and why some people might disagree with you.

Phil Willis, the Liberal Democrat MP for Harrogate.

Sample programme – *The Sunday Edition*

On 27 December 2006, *The Sunday Edition*, which is an ITV politics programme, broadcast an episode on the nature of religion. The programme featured a discussion between Tony Benn, a Christian agnostic and ex-Labour minister, and Richard Dawkins, an outspoken atheist, Professor of Biology and author of *The God Delusion*.

If you watched this programme, you would need to note what things were said that might make people disbelieve in God, and what things were said that might make people believe in God. You would then need to decide what you thought about the programme and why.

Sample programme – *Only Fools and Horses*

In the episode The Miracle of Peckham, this classic BBC sitcom investigated the nature of miracles in a very amusing way.

It begins with Del Boy going to church to confess his sin of handling stolen goods. The priest begins to voice his doubts about God's existence, because the church hospice is being closed down unless they can raise £1 million and the old and sick will not be able to be near their relatives. As Del Boy leaves the church the statue of the Virgin Mary starts crying. By selling the TV and newspaper rights to the miracle they raise the money for the hospice. Later we learn that the stolen goods were the lead from the church roof and the tears of the Virgin were the rain coming through the roof. However, the money for the hospice was raised by Del Boy who did not keep any for himself.

If you had watched this programme, you would need to note what happened and what was said that might encourage people to believe in God. You would then need to note what happened and what was said that might encourage some people not to believe in God. Finally, you would need to decide how the programme affected your beliefs about God. Remember you need evidence for your point of view and why some people might disagree with you.

A Seaside Parish was a fly-on-the-wall documentary about the work of a divorced, re-married woman priest, Reverend Christine Musser, as the new vicar of Boscastle, an insular coastal village in Cornwall with a thriving pagan, as well as Christian, community. It proved surprisingly popular and is now into its third series.

Questions

b Do you think programmes about religion can affect your belief in God? Give two reasons for your point of view. **4**

c Choose one programme about religion and explain how it might affect someone's belief about God. **8**

d 'Religious programmes on television or the radio encourage you to believe in God.'
  i Do you agree? Give reasons for your opinion. **3**
  ii Give reasons why some people may disagree with you. **3**

Exam Tip

d Use the evaluation technique on page 9. Evidence for your own opinion will come from your notes about how the programme affected your attitude to belief in God. Evidence for why some people might disagree with you will come from your notes on the programme either on how it encouraged or how it discouraged belief in God.

SUMMARY

You need to study two programmes about religion. For each one you will need to know:

- an outline of its contents
- how it might have encouraged some people to believe in God
- how it might have encouraged some people not to believe in God
- whether it affected your beliefs about God.

How to answer exam questions

Question A What is atheism?   2 marks

Atheism is believing that there is no God.

Question B Do you think God is the cause of the universe?
Give two reasons for your point of view.   4 marks

Yes I do think that God is the cause of the universe because everything needs a cause and God is the only thing that could have created something as big as the universe. Also I am a Christian and it is one of the beliefs of Christianity that God created the universe. In fact it says so in the creed.

Question C Explain how a religious upbringing can lead to, or support, belief in God.   8 marks

Christians usually teach their children to pray to God. This will make the children believe that God exists because otherwise their parents would not want them to pray to him. If God did not exist, they and their parents would not waste their time praying to nothing. Also they may feel God's presence when they pray. So because they've been brought up to pray, they believe that God must exist.

Another feature of a Christian upbringing is going to church. When children go to church they see lots of people praying to God and worshipping God and this is bound to make them think that God must exist because all these people believe he does.

Many Christian parents also send their children to a Church school. Here they will have RE lessons which teach them that God exists and the children are likely to believe it because their teachers tell them it is true.

Question D 'Considering the evidence, everyone should be an agnostic.'

  i Do you agree? Give reasons for your opinion.   3 marks
  ii Give reasons why some people may disagree with you.   3 marks

i I do not agree because I am an atheist, not an agnostic. I think that science, the Big Bang, DNA and evolution are compelling proof that God does not exist because he did not create the universe or people. Also if God existed, surely he would have sent only one holy book, he would allow only one religion. Furthermore, the fact of evil and suffering in the world proves that God does not exist, because an all-good and all-powerful being would not allow it. The evidence of science, the problem of evil and suffering, and the huge problems of different religions convince me that there is no God and so I disagree with the statement.

ii I can see why some people would disagree with me because evidence such as design can be used both for and against God's existence. The Design Argument seems to prove God's existence, but the Big Bang seems to disprove it. In the same way the First Cause argument seems to prove God's existence, but then there is the question of what caused God. Then the religious evidence to prove God's existence such as miracles, holy books etc., can be explained in non-religious ways. So, it seems logical to say there is not enough evidence either way, so they are agnostics.

QUESTION A
High marks because it is a correct definition.

QUESTION B
A high mark answer because an opinion is backed up by two developed reasons.

QUESTION C
A high mark answer because it begins with a developed reason on how being taught to pray leads to belief in God. This is backed up by two further reasons – going to worship and going to a church school. It is written in a formal style of English in sentences and paragraphs. The spelling is good and it uses specialist vocabulary such as prayer, worship, church, God's presence.

QUESTION D
A high mark answer because it states the candidate's own opinion and backs it up with three clear reasons for thinking that the evidence for atheism is greater than the evidence for agnosticism. It then gives three reasons for people disagreeing and believing that the evidence shows that everyone should be agnostic.

Section 2 **Matters of life and death**

Introduction

This section of the examination specification requires you to look at issues surrounding life after death, abortion, euthanasia, and the media and matters of life and death.

Life after death
You will need to understand the effects of, and give reasons for your own opinion about:
- why Christians believe in life after death and how this belief affects their lives
- why the followers of one religion other than Christianity believe in life after death and how this belief affects their lives
- non-religious reasons for believing in life after death (near-death experiences, ghosts, mediums, the evidence of reincarnation)
- why some people do not believe in life after death.

Abortion
You will need to understand the effects of, and give reasons for your own opinion about:
- the nature of abortion, including current UK legislation, and non-religious arguments about abortion
- different Christian attitudes to abortion and the reasons for them
- different attitudes to abortion in one religion other than Christianity and the reasons for them.

Euthanasia
You will need to understand the effects of, and give reasons for your own opinion about:
- the nature of euthanasia including current British legislation, and non-religious arguments about euthanasia
- different Christian attitudes to euthanasia and the reasons for them
- different attitudes to euthanasia in one religion other than Christianity and the reasons for them.

The media and matters of life and death
You will need to understand the effects of, and give reasons for your own opinion about, arguments over whether the media should or should not be free to criticise religious attitudes to matters of life and death.

Topic 2.1 Christian beliefs about life after death

KEY WORDS

Immortality of the soul – the idea that the soul lives on after the death of the body.

Paranormal – unexplained things which are thought to have spiritual causes, for example, ghosts, mediums.

Resurrection – the belief that, after death, the body stays in the grave until the end of the world, when it is raised.

For what I received I passed on to you as of first importance: that Christ died for our sins according to the Scriptures, that he was buried, that he was raised on the third day according to the Scriptures and that he appeared to Peter, and then to the Twelve … But if it is preached that Christ has been raised from the dead, how can some of you say that there is no resurrection of the dead … For as in Adam all die, so in Christ all will be made alive.

1 Corinthians 15: 3–5, 12, 22

Why Christians believe in life after death

Christians believe that this life is not all there is. They believe God will reward the good and punish the bad in some form of life after death. Although there are different views about what happens after death among Christians, all Christians believe in life after death because:

- The main Christian belief is that Jesus rose from the dead. All four **Gospels** record that Jesus was crucified and buried in a stone tomb. They also record that, on the Sunday morning, some of his women disciples went to the tomb and found it empty. The Gospels then record different 'resurrection appearances' of Jesus. The rest of the New Testament is full of references to the resurrection of Jesus. Clearly, if Jesus rose from the dead, then there is life after death.
- St Paul teaches in 1 Corinthians 15 that people will have a resurrection like that of Jesus, and will have a spiritual resurrection body given to them by God.
- **John the Divine** teaches in Revelation that, at the end of the world, the dead will be raised and brought before God for judgement. Good Christians will enter heaven, everyone else will go to hell.
- Jesus taught that he would come again at the end of the world for a final judgement resulting in heaven or hell.
- The major creeds of the Church teach that Jesus rose from the dead and that there will be life after death. Christians are supposed to believe the creeds and so they should believe in life after death.
- All the Christian Churches teach that there is life after death. **Protestant**, Catholic, **Orthodox** and **Pentecostal** Churches may have some differences about what they think life after death will be like, but they all teach their followers that there will be life after death. Therefore Christians should believe in life after death.

*I believe in …
the resurrection of the body and the life everlasting.*

Apostles' Creed

- Many Christians believe that people are made up of a body (physical) and a soul (mind or personality). They believe that the soul is non-material and immortal (will never die). They believe that when the body dies, the soul leaves the body to live with God.

- Many Christians believe in life after death because it gives their lives meaning and purpose. They feel that for life to end at death does not make sense. A life after death, in which people will be judged on how they live this life with the good rewarded and the evil punished, makes sense of this life. If the purpose of life is to live your life in such a way that you spend eternity in heaven, then that gives life meaning.
- Some Christians believe in life after death because of the evidence of the **paranormal** (see Topic 2.3, page 42).

Some Christians believe that the tunnel of light seen in near-death experiences is evidence that heaven exists. Do you agree?

Jesus links faith in the resurrection to his own person: 'I am the Resurrection and the life.' It is Jesus himself who on the Last Day will raise up those who have believed in him.

Catechism of the Catholic Church 994

'I think, therefore I am.'

This famous statement by the philosopher Descartes is used by some Christians to show that the mind is separate from, and greater than, the body. They claim this means the mind can live without the body, and so they believe in the **immortality of the soul.**

How Christian beliefs about life after death affect the lives of Christians

1 Christians believe that what happens to them after they die will be determined by how they have lived this life. Many Christians believe that they will be judged by God and that only if they have lived a good Christian life will they be allowed into heaven.

This means that Christians will try to live a good Christian life following the teachings of the Bible and the Church so that they go to heaven and not hell when they die.

2 Living a good Christian life will mean following the teachings of Jesus who taught that the two greatest commandments are to love God and to love your neighbour as yourself. So Christians' lives will be affected as they try to love God by praying and by worshipping God. Catholic Christians will try to attend **Mass** every Sunday, most other Christians will also try to worship in church once a week.

3 Trying to love your neighbour as yourself is bound to affect a Christian's life. In the parable of the Sheep and Goats (Matthew 25:31–46), Jesus said that only those who fed the hungry, clothed the naked, befriended strangers, visited the sick and those in prison, would be allowed into heaven. Those who ignored all these people's needs would be sent to hell at the final judgement.

This is a similar teaching to the Good Samaritan (Luke 10:29–37) where Jesus taught that loving your neighbour means helping anyone in need. These teachings are bound to affect Christians' lives and explain why Christian charities like Christian Aid and CAFOD are so involved in helping those in need.

4 Christians believe that sin can prevent people from going to heaven. Some Christians believe that those who die with unforgiven sins will go to hell. The Catholic Church teaches that those who die with unforgiven sins will go to purgatory to be purified before they can reach heaven. Clearly these teachings mean that Christians will try to avoid committing sins in their lives so that they will go to heaven.

The Parable of the Good Samaritan

'Which of these three do you think was a neighbour to the man who fell into the hands of robbers?' The expert in the law replied, 'The one who had mercy on him.'

Luke 10:36–37

Every action of yours, every thought, should be those of one who expects to die before the day is out. Death would have no terrors for you if you had a quiet conscience.

The Imitation of Christ by Thomas à Kempis (a medieval saint)

5 Christian beliefs about life after death give their lives meaning and purpose. Living life with a purpose and believing that this life has meaning, both affect the way that Christians live. It may be why in surveys Christians suffer less from depression and are less likely to commit suicide than atheists and agnostics.

How does a necropolis (city of the dead), like this in Glasgow, show Christian belief in life after death?

Questions

b Do you think Christians are right to believe in life after death? Give two reasons for your point of view. **4**

c Explain why Christians believe in life after death. **8**

d 'Christians only believe in life after death because they're scared of dying.'
  i Do you agree? Give reasons for your opinion. **3**
  ii Give reasons why some people may disagree with you. **3**

Exam Tip

c 'Explain' means give reasons. To answer this question you should use four reasons from this section, and make each of them into a short paragraph. For tips on Quality of Written Communication, look at page 3.

SUMMARY

Christians believe in life after death because:
- Jesus rose from the dead
- the Bible and the Creeds say there is life after death
- the Church teaches that there is life after death
- the soul is something that can never die.

Their beliefs about life after death affect their lives because Christians will try to love God and love their neighbour so that they go to heaven and not hell.

Topic 2.2.1 Islam and life after death

Why Muslims believe in life after death

Muslims believe in life after death because:

- The **Qur'an** teaches that there is life after death. Muslims believe that the Qur'an is the word of God which contains everything God wants humans to know, therefore they must believe whatever the Qur'an says.
- Muhammad taught that there is life after death. Muslims believe that the **Prophet Muhammad** is the last prophet God will ever send and the perfect example for Muslims. Therefore they must believe whatever he taught.
- Islam has six fundamental beliefs (belief in: Allah, his angels, his holy books, his messengers, the Last Day and life after death) which all Muslims are expected to believe. Since Muhammad said all Muslims must believe these, Muslims must believe in life after death.
- Muslims believe that this life is a test from God. The idea of a test involves the need for a judgement as to how you have done in the test, and rewards for those who pass. Judgement and reward can only happen if there is life after death, therefore Muslims believe in life after death because it makes sense of this life being a test.
- Many Muslims believe in life after death because it gives their lives meaning and purpose. They feel that for life to end at death does not make sense. A life after death, in which people will be judged on how they live this life with the good rewarded and the evil punished, makes sense of this life. If the purpose of life is to live your life in such a way that you spend eternity in heaven, then that gives life meaning.

Because of their beliefs about life after death, Muslims are never cremated. They are buried (facing **Makkah**) as soon as possible with no organs removed from the body.

How Muslim beliefs about life after death affect the lives of Muslims

1 Islam teaches that on the Last Day, all humans will be gathered before God on a vast plain (most Muslims believe this will be the plain of **Arafat**) and judged by God. The judgement will be made on the nature of people's lives. Those who have lived good Muslim lives will pass the judgement and go to paradise, everyone else will fail and go to hell. This affects Muslims' lives because they must try to live good Muslim lives if they are to go to paradise and avoid hell.

2 Living a good Muslim life means observing the **Five Pillars** of Islam. So belief in life after death means that Muslims will pray five times a day, they will fast during **Ramadan**, they will pay their **zakah** and they will go on **hajj** at least once. So their beliefs about life after death will have a big effect on their lives.

3 Living a good Muslim life also means following the holy law of Islam, the **Shari'ah**. This will affect a Muslim's life because they will have to eat **halal** food, observe Muslim dress laws, not drink alcohol, not gamble or be involved in lending at or receiving interest, etc.

4 Muslims believe that resurrection means that nothing should be removed from the body after death. This means that funerals take place within 48 hours and the body is simply embalmed and buried. This affects Muslim lives because they try to avoid post-mortems and many Muslims have concerns about transplant surgery.

5 Muslim beliefs about life after death give their lives meaning and purpose. Living life with a purpose and believing that this life has meaning, both affect the way that Muslims live. It may be why in surveys Muslims suffer less from depression and are less likely to commit suicide than atheists and agnostics.

Muslims prepare for the Last Day when they confess their sins at Arafat.

> *Let him who believes in Allah and the Last Day either speak good or keep silent, and let him who believes in Allah and the Last Day be generous to his neighbour, and let him who believes in Allah and the Last Day be generous to his guest.*
>
> **Hadith recorded by al'Bukhari and Muslim**

Questions

b Do you believe in life after death? Give two reasons for your point of view. **4**

c Choose one religion other than Christianity and explain how its beliefs about life after death affect the lives of its followers. **8**

d 'Your soul will never die.'

  i Do you agree? Give reasons for your opinion. **3**

  ii Give reasons why some people may disagree with you. **3**

Exam Tip

c Remember to say which religion you have chosen. 'Explain' means give reasons. To answer this question you should name four Muslim beliefs about life after death and explain, in two or three sentences for each, how they might affect a Muslim's life. For tips on Quality of Written Communication, look at page 3.

SUMMARY

Muslims believe in life after death because it is taught in the Qur'an, in the **hadith** of the Prophet and is one of the essential six beliefs of Islam.

Their beliefs about life after death affect their lives because Muslims will try to follow the Five Pillars and the teachings of the Shari'ah so that they go to heaven and not hell.

Topic 2.2.2 Judaism and life after death

> *I believe with perfect faith that there will be a resurrection of the dead at a time when it will please the Creator, blessed be His name.*
>
> **Number 13 of The Thirteen Principles of Faith**

Why Jewish people believe in life after death

Jewish people believe in life after death because:

- It is the teaching of the **Tenakh**. Jews believe that the first five books of the Tenakh (the **Torah**) are a direct communication from God which must be believed. The other books of the Tenakh are inspired by God. Therefore Jews should believe what the Tenakh says.
- It is the teaching of the **Talmud**. The Talmud is a collection of the Oral Torah, discussions by **rabbis** about the laws of the Torah, which most Jews try to follow.
- It is one of the **Thirteen Principles of Faith** that are described in the Daily Prayer Book as 'Articles of the Jewish Creed'. As part of the creed, Jews would feel they should believe it.
- Many Jews believe in life after death because it gives their lives meaning and purpose. They feel that for life to end at death does not make sense. A life after death, in which people will be judged on how they live this life with the good rewarded and the evil punished, makes sense of this life. If the purpose of life is to live your life in such a way that you spend eternity in heaven, then that gives life meaning.
- Some Jews believe in life after death because of the evidence of the paranormal (see Topic 2.3, page 42).

How Jewish beliefs about life after death affect the lives of Jewish people

1 The main teaching of Judaism about life after death is resurrection. Based on the Torah and Tenakh, the Thirteen Principles of Faith state that God will end this world when he decides so to do. Then he will create a new world and resurrect the dead. God will decide what happens to people on the basis of how they have lived their lives. This life after death will be true life, so Jewish cemeteries are called 'the House of Life'. This affects the lives of Jewish people because they must try to live good Jewish lives if they are to have a good life after death.

> *Because of it I clothed Lebanon with gloom, and all the trees of the field withered away. I made the nations tremble at the sound of its fall when I brought it down to the grave with those who go down to the pit.*
>
> **Ezekiel 31:15–16**

2 Living a good Jewish life means observing the Torah and **halakhah** for **Orthodox Jews**. So belief in life after death means that Orthodox Jews will pray three times a day, they will fast on **Yom Kippur**, they will observe the laws of **Shabbat**, and they will celebrate the many festivals. Therefore their beliefs about life after death will have a big effect on their lives.

3 Living a good Jewish life also means following all the **mitzvot** as set out in the halakhah. This will affect a Jewish person's life because they will have to keep **kosher**, observe the dress laws, and not be involved in lending at or receiving interest, etc.

4 Orthodox Jews believe that they should make a final confession and recite the **shema** before they die. They also have a duty to help with funerals and to keep **shiva**. This affects the lives of Jewish people because they are always aware of the proximity of death.

5 Jewish beliefs about life after death give their lives meaning and purpose. Living life with a purpose and believing that this life has meaning, both affect the way that Jewish people live. It may be why in surveys religious Jews suffer less from depression and are less likely to commit suicide than atheists and agnostics.

A Jewish cemetery at Southgate, London. Why is this called the House of Life?

In the last days the mountain of the Lord's temple will be established as chief among the mountains; it will be raised above the hills, and all nations will stream to it.

Isaiah 2:2

Questions

b Do you believe in life after death? Give two reasons for your point of view. **4**

c Choose one religion other than Christianity and explain how its beliefs about life after death affect the lives of its followers. **8**

d 'Your soul will never die.'
  i Do you agree? Give reasons for your opinion. **3**
  ii Give reasons why some people may disagree with you. **3**

Exam Tip

c Remember to say which religion you have chosen. 'Explain' means give reasons. To answer this question you should name four Jewish beliefs about life after death and explain, in two or three sentences for each, how they might affect a Jew's life. For tips on Quality of Written Communication, look at page 3.

SUMMARY

Jewish people believe in life after death because it is the teaching of the Tenakh and Talmud, and is one of the Thirteen Principles of Faith.

Their beliefs about life after death affect their lives because Orthodox Jews will try to follow the halakhah so that they go to heaven and not hell.

Topic 2.2.3 Hinduism and life after death

Why Hindus believe in life after death

Hindus believe in life after death because:

- It is taught in the **Vedas**. The Vedas are called shruti texts, which means that they have been revealed by **Brahman** and so contain eternal truths that most Hindus believe.
- It is taught in the **Upanishads**, which many Hindus also believe to be shruti texts and which they should therefore believe.
- It is taught in the **Bhagavad Gita**, which is the most popular of Hindu scriptures. Many Hindus feel that the teachings of the Gita contain ultimate truths and so must be believed.
- Many Hindus believe in life after death because it gives their lives meaning and purpose. They feel that for life to end at death does not make sense. **Reincarnation** rewards the good and punishes the evil, but also gives everyone a second chance. Hindus feel that this makes sense of this life.
- Hindus also believe in life after death because of the evidence for reincarnation, for example children who are born knowing things they could not know unless they had been on earth before. This is a further reason for Hindus to believe in life after death (see Topic 2.3, page 42).

> **KEY WORD**
>
> Reincarnation – the belief that, after death, souls are reborn in a new body.

> *What a man becomes in his next life depends upon his* **karma.** *By good deeds he attains merit, by bad actions he becomes evil. The karma of a man ruled by desire attaches to his atman, so that he is forced to suffer rebirth and return to the world of men. When all attachment arising from desire is destroyed, man's mortality ends and only then does atman reach Brahman.*
>
> Upanishads IV.4:3–5

The Gita records that in his meeting with **Krishna**, the soldier, Arjuna, learned about the nature of the soul and rebirth.

How Hindu beliefs about life after death affect the lives of Hindus

1 Hinduism teaches that each person has an immortal **atman**, which travels through many lives in different bodies. The body it is reborn into is dependent on the state of the soul: the better the soul the better life the body will have. The aim of life is to escape from this process of **samsara** and gain **moksha**. Moksha is liberation from rebirth and when the soul gains moksha, it will not be reborn. Instead it will live in a state of bliss, free from sorrow and free from desire. This state of bliss is often called **nirvana**. This affects the lives of Hindus because they must try to live the type of life that will lead them to moksha.

2 The lives of some Hindus are very affected because they believe that the way to gain moksha is by karma yoga – following your duty (**dharma**). This means that they follow all the rules of the four stages of life (**ashrama**) in order to reach moksha.

3 These Hindus believe that whatever happens to them in this life is because of how they behaved in previous lives (the **law of karma**) and so they try to make sure that they only do things in this life that will bring good effects in their next life.

4 Some Hindus believe that the way to gain moksha is by devotion to Krishna, or one of the other **avatars** of the divine (bhakti yoga). Such Hindus will spend a lot of time in worship (**puja**) both at home and in the **mandir**. They will also go on pilgrimage to places connected with the avatar.

5 Some Hindus believe that moksha is achieved through deep meditation to achieve oneness with Brahman (jnana yoga). This has a huge effect on their lives because deep meditation requires isolation from relationships with people in order to spend sufficient time in meditation.

Many Hindus follow both karma yoga and bhakti yoga so their beliefs about life after death have a huge effect on their lives.

Finite they say are these our bodies indwelt by an eternal embodied soul – a soul indestructible ... As a man casts off his worn out clothes and takes on other new ones in their place, so does the embodied soul cast off his worn out bodies and enters others anew ... For sure is the death of all that comes to birth, sure the birth of all that dies.

Bhagavad Gita 2:18, 22, 27

A Hindu cremation on the banks of the River Ganges in India. Why are Hindus cremated?

SUMMARY
Hindus believe in life after death because it is the teaching of the Vedas, Upanishads and Gita. Their beliefs about life after death affect their lives because they will try to gain moksha either by living a good life, or living a life devoted to God or by living a life of meditation.

Topic 2.2.4 Sikhism and life after death

Why Sikhs believe in life after death

Sikhs believe in life after death because:

- It is taught in the **Guru Granth Sahib**. Sikhs regard the Guru Granth Sahib as their living Guru. They believe it contains all the important teachings of the **Ten Gurus** and so must be believed. Many Sikhs regard the Guru Granth Sahib as the words of God.

- It is clear that the Ten Gurus all believed in life after death. Sikhs believe that they should follow both the examples and the teachings of the human Gurus, and so they should believe in life after death.

- Sikhs believe that God would not have created humans without an ultimate purpose. He would not have created humans just to live this life and then die. A good God is bound to have created a life after death for his creatures.

- Many Sikhs believe in life after death because it gives their lives meaning and purpose. They feel that for life to end at death does not make sense. Reincarnation (sse page 38) rewards the good and punishes the evil, but also gives everyone a second chance. Sikhs feel that this makes sense of this life.

- Sikhs also believe in life after death because of the evidence for reincarnation, for example children who are born knowing things they could not know unless they had been on earth before. This is a further reason for Sikhs to believe in life after death (see Topic 2.3, page 42).

> *Know the real purpose of being here, gather up treasure under the True Guru's guidance. Make your mind God's home. If God abides with you undisturbed, you will not be reborn.*
>
> **Guru Granth Sahib 13**

> *Humanity is brimful of the nectar of God's name. Through tasting it, its relish is known. Those who taste it become free from fear and find that God's elixir satisfies their needs. Whoever is made to drink it through divine grace is never again afflicted by death.*
>
> **Guru Granth Sahib 1092**

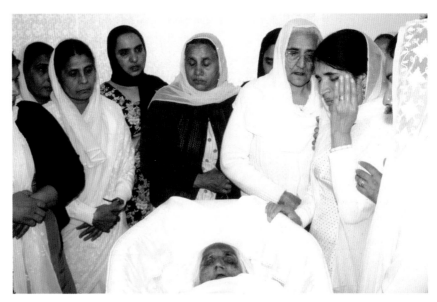

The Sikh funeral service says, 'The dawn of a new day is the herald of a sunset. Earth is not your permanent home.'
Guru Granth Sahib 793

How Sikh beliefs about life after death affect the lives of Sikhs

Sikhism teaches that there is 'a divine spark' in every human being, which is a part of God. Souls are reborn (**samsara**) until they have attained sufficient purity to attain **mukti**, release from rebirth. Sikhism teaches that the way to mukti is through moving from being **manmukh** (human-centred) to being **gurmukh** (God-centred). The way to be God-centred has been shown by the Ten Gurus and the Guru Granth Sahib. The souls of the human-centred will always be reborn, but the souls of the God-centred will achieve release from rebirth. This is bound to affect a Sikh's life as they try to follow the teachings on how to be gurmukh.

How does the way the Guru Granth Sahib is being treated show that Sikhs should believe what their holy book says about life after death?

Questions

b Do you believe in life after death? Give two reasons for your point of view. **4**

c Choose one religion other than Christianity and explain how its beliefs about life after death affect the lives of its followers. **8**

d 'Your soul will never die.'

   i Do you agree? Give reasons for your opinion. **3**

   ii Give reasons why some people may disagree with you. **3**

Exam Tip

c Remember to say which religion you have chosen. 'Explain' means give reasons. To answer this question you should name four Sikh beliefs about life after death and explain, in two or three sentences for each, how they might affect a Sikh's life. For tips on Quality of Written Communication, look at page 3.

SUMMARY

Sikhs believe in life after death because it is the teaching of the Guru Granth Sahib and the Ten Gurus.

Their beliefs about life after death affect their lives because they will try to gain mukti by living a good life which is God-centred.

Topic 2.3 Non-religious reasons for believing in life after death

Non-religious reasons for believing in life after death are connected to evidence for the paranormal. This can refer to a wide range of things from ghosts to telekinesis (moving objects without touching them). However, there are three main parts of the paranormal that provide reasons for believing in life after death:

1. Near-death experiences

This is a fairly recent phenomenon and happens when people are clinically dead for a period of time and then come back to life. In his research, Dr Sam Parnia of Southampton General Hospital found that four out of 63 patients who had survived a heart attack had **near-death experiences**. Similar research in Holland by Dr Pim van Lommel, in the USA by Dr Raymond Moody and elsewhere in Britain by Dr Peter Fenwick and Dr Sue Blackmore, produced similar results.

Frequently quoted in near-death experiences are: feelings of peace and joy; feelings of floating above the body; seeing a bright light; entering another world; meeting dead relatives; coming to a point of no return.

Example of evidence of a near-death experience

Jeanette Mitchell-Meadows had such an experience when she was undergoing major spinal surgery. She felt herself leaving her body and following a bright light to what she thought was heaven. It was very peaceful, she heard music more clear and tuneful than anything on earth and then she felt she met Jesus. She met her grandparents and her daughter, who had been killed in an accident about six months earlier. She did not want to leave, but was told God had things for her to do on earth. When she returned to her body she felt great pain.

Clearly, if near-death experiences are true then some people may see this as evidence that there is a heaven and there is life after death.

2. Evidence for a spirit world

Ghosts and ouija boards appear to give evidence of the spirits or souls of the dead surviving death, but the clearest evidence seems to come from mediums.

A medium is a person who claims to have the gift of communicating between the material world in which we live and the spirit world inhabited by those who have died. They are sometimes called psychics, clairvoyants or spirit guides.

This research is very good work, which is needed to understand the near-death experience, but it proves absolutely nothing about the soul. All claims about this being evidence for consciousness existing without a brain are unfounded, baseless rubbish.

Dr Sue Blackmore

We know that memories are extremely fallible. We are quite good at knowing that something happened, but we are very poor at knowing when it happened. It is quite possible that these experiences happened during the recovery or just before the cardiac arrest. To say that they happened when the brain was shut down, I think there is little evidence for that at all.

Dr Chris Freeman, Consultant Psychiatrist

Mediums exist in all countries and all religions, though they have become more publicised recently. Living TV regularly features mediums in programmes such as: *Street Psychic, Beyond with James van Praagh*, and *Crossing Over with John Edward*.

There are many TV shows featuring mediums. Two of the most famous are Craig and Jane Hamilton-Parker, who claim they met through Craig contacting the spirit of Jane's dead grandmother.

Most mediums claim that the founders of the world religions (such as Buddha, Jesus and Muhammad) were in touch with the spirit world, and that religions point to the spirit world rather than having absolute truth. They claim that God is beyond religion and that spirits have second chances to make up for their mistakes whether through reincarnation or development in the spirit world.

Mediums claim to provide evidence for life after death by contacting people's dead relatives and telling them things only their relatives could know.

Example of evidence for the spirit world

The medium Stephen O'Brien told Marion Jones that he could see a peasant grandmother figure sitting on a rickety chair outside a wooden shack. She was nodding and looking very happy. Then she told Stephen that she was thanking Marion for helping her grandson and she was speaking the word Cruz. Stephen thought perhaps there was a South American connection. Marion realised that Cruz was the surname of a 10-year-old Mexican boy whose education and health she was sponsoring. She was sure that Stephen O'Brien had contacted the boy's grandmother in the spirit world and had information he could not possibly have known.

If mediums can contact the dead in a spirit world, then there must be a life after death.

Robert Thouless (President of the Society for Psychical Research) made an encrypted message before he died that would allow mediums to prove that they had contacted him after his death. At least 100 mediums submitted keys to the cypher, but none were correct, whereas a computer program solved it easily. A simple explanation is that Thouless had not survived death and so could not be contacted by mediums.

Adapted from *The Case Against Immortality* by Keith Augustine

The theory that mediums communicate with discarnate intelligences becomes even more suspect in the light of experiments in which mediumistic contact has been made with living or demonstrably fictional characters.

From *Paranormal Experiences and Survival of Death* by C. Becker

Baby with tail who some Hindus believe to be a reincarnation of a Hindu god.

In only eleven of the approximate 1,111 rebirth cases had there been no contact between the two families before an investigation was begun. Of these, seven were seriously flawed in some respect ... The rebirth cases are anecdotal evidence of the weakest sort.

From *Immortality* by Paul Edwards

3. The evidence of reincarnation

Hindus, Sikhs and Buddhists believe that life after death involves souls being reborn into another body. There are many stories of this in India, one of the most famous being reported in July 2002 at the National Conference of Forensic Science in India.

Example of reincarnation

In 1996, Taranjit Singh was born to a poor peasant family and received no education. From the age of two he claimed he had a previous life and had been killed by a motor scooter on 10 September 1992. His present parents took him to the village he said he came from and the village teacher confirmed the accident had happened and introduced him to his original parents whom he recognised. The forensic scientist, Vikram Chauhan, checked the first boy's education and asked Taranjit to write the English and Punjabi alphabets (even though Taranjit had never been taught them). Not only could he write them, but when Vikram tested his handwriting against that of the dead boy, he found they were identical.

Example of reincarnation

Crowds are flocking to Indian temples to see a Muslim baby with a tail who is believed to be the reincarnation of a Hindu god. The 11-month-old boy has been named Balaji, another name for monkey-faced Lord Hanuman. He is reported to have a four-inch tail caused by genetic mutations during the development of the foetus. Iqbal Qureshi, the child's maternal grandfather, is taking Balaji from temple to temple where people offer money to see the boy. Mr Qureshi says the baby has nine spots on his body like Lord Hanuman and has shown them to journalists.

Source: *The Tribune of India*, 2003

If this is true, then it would be evidence for reincarnation, and so life after death.

SUMMARY

Some people believe in life after death for non-religious reasons such as:

- near-death experiences when people see things during heart attacks, operations, etc.
- evidence of the spirit world, ghosts, mediums, etc.
- evidence of reincarnation, such as people remembering previous lives.

Questions

b Do you think that some people see ghosts? Give two reasons for your point of view. **4**

c Explain why some people believe that the paranormal proves there is life after death. **8**

d 'The paranormal proves that there is life after death.'
  i Do you agree? Give reasons for your opinion. **3**
  ii Give reasons why some people may disagree with you. **3**

Exam Tip

d Use the answering evaluation questions advice from page 9. The arguments for can be found in this topic. The arguments against could be the quotes in the margin from Sue Blackmore, Chris Freeman, Keith Augustine and Paul Edwards. You could also use some of the arguments from Topic 2.4, page 45.

Topic 2.4 Why some people do not believe in life after death

Not all people believe in life after death. Many people who do not believe in God believe this life is all there is, and, just like animals and plants, humans cease to exist when they die.

They believe this because:

- If there is no God, there is nothing non-material. There is no heaven to go to after death.
- The different religions have different ideas about life after death, whereas, if it were true, they would all say the same things about it. This is especially true of the difference between the reincarnation ideas of Hinduism, Buddhism and Sikhism and the one life leading to judgement and heaven and hell of Judaism, Christianity and Islam.
- The evidence for life after death is either based on holy books, and there is no way for a non-believer to decide which holy book should be believed, or the paranormal, which has been criticised by scientists.
- Most beliefs in life after death assume that the mind or soul can survive without the body. But the evidence of science is that the human mind developed as the brain grew more complex, and so the mind cannot exist without the brain (for example, people who are brain dead on a life-support machine).
- There is nowhere for life after death to take place. Space exploration has shown there is no heaven above the sky and physics has shown there is no non-material world on earth. Where, then, could life after death take place?
- We can only recognise people by their bodies, so how would we recognise souls without bodies? If souls survive death, then they would be alone with no way of contacting other souls, which would not really be life after death.
- Some people have been brought up not to believe in life after death either because their parents are not religious, or because their parents' experience of the death of loved ones is that there is nothing after death.

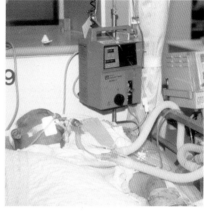

Does a person whose brain is dead still have a mind or soul?

SUMMARY

Some people do not believe in life after death because:

- they do not believe in God
- there is no scientific evidence
- they do not see where life after death could take place.

Questions

b Do you believe there can be a life after death?
  Give two reasons for your point of view. **4**

c Explain why some people do not believe in life after death. **8**

d 'When you're dead, you're dead and that's the end of you.'
  i Do you agree? Give reasons for your opinion. **3**
  ii Give reasons why some people may disagree with you. **3**

Exam Tip

c 'Explain' means give reasons. To answer this question you should use four reasons from this topic, and make each of them into a short paragraph. For tips on Quality of Written Communication, look at page 3.

Topic 2.5 The nature of abortion

Statistics

Number of abortions carried out in England and Wales

1971	94,570
1995	154,315
1999	173,701
2001	176,364
2006	193,700

(89 per cent carried out at under 13 weeks' gestation)

Source: Office of National Statistics

Pro-choice is the name given to those who support a woman's right to abortion. They do not want women to risk their lives by having operations carried out by non-doctors in bad conditions.

United Kingdom law on abortion

The 1967 Act states that an **abortion** can be carried out if two doctors agree that:

- the mother's life is at risk
- there is a risk of injury to the mother's physical or mental health
- there is a risk that another child would put at risk the mental or physical health of existing children
- there is a substantial risk that the baby might be born seriously handicapped.

The 1990 Act states that abortions cannot take place after 24 weeks of pregnancy, unless the mother's life is gravely at risk or the foetus is likely to be born with severe mental or physical abnormalities, because advances in medical techniques mean that such foetuses have a chance of survival.

Why abortion is a controversial issue

Abortion is a controversial issue because there are so many different issues about abortion itself:

- Many religions, and anti-abortion groups (many of which are religious), believe that life begins at the moment of conception when the male sperm and the female ovum combine. Therefore abortion is wrong because it is taking a human life.
- Many people believe that a baby cannot be considered as a separate life until it is capable of living outside the mother. Therefore abortions before a certain length of pregnancy are not taking life.

- Many non-religious people believe that a woman should have the right to do what she wants with her own body in the same way that men do. They would argue that an unwanted pregnancy is no different from an unwanted tumour. The problems caused to a woman by having an unwanted baby justify her having an abortion.
- Many religious people believe that the unborn child's rights supersede those of the mother and that both the father and the child have claims on the mother's body.
- Some people argue that because foetuses born at 22–24 weeks can now survive, the time limit for abortions should be reduced to 18 or 20 weeks.
- There are also arguments about whether medical staff should have to carry out abortions. Some people argue that they should not be made to act against their conscience; others argue that abortion is just a medical procedure like any other.

Pro-life is the name given to those who support the foetus' right to life and want abortion banned because it denies the foetus' right to life.

If carrying out a particular procedure or giving advice about it conflicts with your religious or moral beliefs, and this conflict might affect the treatment or advice you provide, you must explain this to the patient and tell them they have the right to see another doctor. You must be satisfied that the patient has sufficient information to enable them to exercise that right. If it is not practical for a patient to arrange to see another doctor, you must ensure that arrangements are made for another suitably qualified colleague to take over your role.

You must not express to your patients your personal beliefs, including political, religious or moral beliefs, in ways that exploit their vulnerability or that are likely to cause them distress.

Advice to doctors from *Personal Beliefs and Medical Practice* published by the General Medical Council 2008

Questions

b Do you agree with abortion? Give two reasons for your point of view.   **4**
c Explain why abortion is a controversial issue.   **8**
d 'Abortion is always wrong.'
  i   Do you agree? Give reasons for your opinion.   **3**
  ii Give reasons why some people may disagree with you.   **3**

Exam Tip

b You should already have thought about this, and you just have to give two reasons for your opinion. For example, if you agree with abortion you could use the reason of the woman's rights over her body and the foetus not being a human life until it can survive outside the womb. If you do not agree with abortion you should use two reasons against abortion from one religion.

SUMMARY

Abortion is allowed in the United Kingdom if two doctors agree that there is medical reason for it.

Abortion is a controversial issue because:

- people disagree about when life begins
- people disagree about whether abortion is murder
- people disagree about whether a woman has the right to choose.

Topic 2.6 Christian attitudes to abortion

Human life must be respected and protected absolutely from the moment of conception. From the first moment of his existence, a human being must be recognised as having the rights of a person – among which is the inviolable right of every innocent being to life ... Abortion and infanticide are abominable crimes ... The law must provide appropriate penal sanctions for every deliberate violation of the child's rights.

Catechism of the Catholic Church 2270–71, 2273

Before I formed you in the womb I knew you, before you were born. I set you apart; I appointed you as a prophet to the nations.

Jeremiah 1:5

Christians have two differing attitudes to abortion:

1 The Catholic Church and **Evangelical Protestant** Churches teach that all abortion is wrong whatever the circumstances because:

- Life is holy and belongs to God, therefore only God has the right to end a pregnancy.
- Life begins at conception. Human life begins when an ovum is fertilised and, as there is no break from conception to birth, abortion is therefore taking life. The Ten Commandments teach that it is wrong to take life, therefore abortion is wrong.
- Every person has a natural 'right to life'. A foetus is a human being and abortion destroys its right to life, so it follows that abortion is wrong.
- These Christians believe there is evidence that women who have abortions can suffer from traumas leading to guilt complexes and sometimes mental illness.
- They also believe that adoption is always a better solution to unwanted pregnancy than abortion as it preserves life and brings joy to a new family.
- Difficult issues surrounding abortion can be dealt with through the doctrine of double effect. If, for example, doctors discover that a pregnant mother has cancer and chemotherapy would kill the foetus, the doctrine of double effect says that the first effect is to save the mother's life, the second (double) effect is to end the life of the foetus; as the death of the foetus is secondary, and so not intended, an abortion has not occurred.
- In the case of a woman becoming pregnant as a result of rape, they believe that one sinful act should not provoke another. With counselling, help and adoption, they believe that good can come out of evil in the form of a new life.

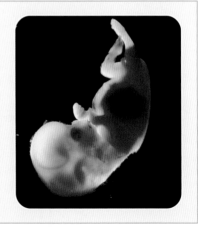

Out of nearly 50 million abortions carried out in the world today, 20 million are unsafe. Ninety per cent of all unsafe abortions take place in developing countries where abortion is restricted by law.

Some 70,000 women die each year as a result of unsafe abortions.

World Health Organisation statistics 2000

2 Other Christians (mainly Liberal Protestants) believe that abortion is wrong, but it must be permitted in certain circumstances such as if the mother has been raped, if the mother's life is at risk or if the foetus is so handicapped that it would have no quality of life. Some of these Christians would also allow abortion for social reasons such as poverty and the effects on the rest of the family. These Christians believe that abortion can be permitted in certain circumstances because:

- Jesus told Christians to love their neighbour as themselves, and abortion may be the most loving thing to do.
- They believe life does not begin at conception.
- The sanctity of life can be broken in such things as a **just war**, so why not in a just abortion?
- Christians should accept technological advances in medicine. Doctors have developed tests for certain medical conditions – like Downs syndrome for example – for unborn babies and so parents should be allowed abortions if such tests show their baby would be born with serious medical problems.
- Christianity is concerned with justice and if abortions were banned, an unjust situation would arise. Rich women would pay for abortions in another country, but the poor would use 'back-street' abortionists.

Some Evangelical Protestants are beginning to change the focus of the abortion debate. The Red Letter Christians (so called because in some Bibles the words of Jesus are printed in red) believe Jesus would have been more concerned about helping the women who want abortions than banning abortions. They think Christians should be making contraception cheaper and more easily available and increasing wages and childcare help for single mothers (70 per cent of abortions in the USA are to women living in poverty).

Methodists would strongly prefer that through advances in medical science and social welfare, all abortions should become unnecessary. But termination as early as possible in the course of pregnancy may be the lesser of evils. If abortion were made a criminal offence again, the result would be 'one law for the rich and another for the poor', with increased risks of ill-health and death as a result of botched 'back-street' abortions.

Statement by the Methodist Church of England and Wales in *What the Churches Say*

Should abortion be legalised in areas like this where thousands of women die as a result of illegal abortions?

Questions

b Do you think abortion is murder? Give two reasons for your point of view. **4**

c Explain why some Christians allow abortion, but some do not. **8**

d 'No Christian should ever have an abortion.'
  i Do you agree? Give reasons for your opinion. **3**
  ii Give reasons why some people may disagree with you. **3**

Exam Tip

c 'Explain why' means give four brief, or two developed, reasons why some Christians do not allow abortion (Catholics and Evangelical Protestants); and four brief, or two developed, reasons why some Christians allow abortion in certain circumstances (Liberal Protestants). For tips on Quality of Written Communication, look at page 3.

SUMMARY

Christians have different attitudes to abortion:

- Some Christians believe that abortion is always wrong because it is murder and against God's will.
- Some Christians believe that abortion is wrong but must be allowed in some circumstances as the lesser of two evils.

Topic 2.7.1 Islam and abortion

> *Kill not your children on a plea of want. We provide sustenance for you and for them; come not nigh to shameful deeds.*
>
> **Surah 6:151**

> *The jurists state that it is permissible to take medicine for abortion as long as the embryo is still unformed in human shape. The period of the unformed shape is given as 120 days. The jurists think that during this state, the embryo is not yet a human being.*
>
> **Fatwa (Islamic legal decision) given by Shayqh Abdullah al'Qalqili**

SUMMARY

- Some Muslims think abortion should never be allowed.
- Some Muslims think abortion can only be allowed if the mother's life is in danger.
- Some Muslims think abortion is allowed until 120 days because this is when the foetus receives its soul.

There are different attitudes to abortion among Muslims.

1 Many Muslims believe that, although abortion should be discouraged, it is permitted up to 120 days of pregnancy. However, they only allow abortion for certain reasons such as: if the mother's life is at risk, the health of the baby is at risk or tests show the baby will be severely handicapped. They have this attitude because:
   - There are several hadith which say that a foetus does not receive its soul until 120 days into the pregnancy, and so is not a human until then.
   - The Shari'ah states that the life of the mother must always take precedence over the life of the child. This is based on the 'lesser of two evils' because the death of the foetus will cause less suffering than the death of the mother.
   - As the foetus is not a human until 120 days, the health of the future baby and its effects on the present family can be taken into consideration until then.

2 Some Muslims believe that abortion is wrong and should never be allowed whatever the circumstances. They have this attitude because:
   - They believe the soul is given at the moment of conception and so the foetus is a human being from conception.
   - The Qur'an says murder is wrong and they think abortion is murder because life begins at conception.
   - They believe that the Qur'an bans abortion.

3 Some Muslims believe that abortion is wrong, but should be used if the mother's life is at risk. They have this attitude because:
   - They believe that the Qur'an bans abortion, but the Shari'ah has laws for when a choice has to be made between the life of the foetus and the life of the mother and says the mother's life comes first.

Questions

b Do you agree with abortion? Give two reasons for your point of view. **4**

c Choose one religion other than Christianity and explain why some of the followers of that religion allow abortion and some do not. **8**

d 'No religious person should ever have an abortion.'
   i Do you agree? Give reasons for your opinion. **3**
   ii Give reasons why some people may disagree with you. **3**

Exam Tip

d Use the answering evaluation questions advice from page 9. The arguments for could be the Muslim reasons for abortion always being wrong plus the Christians reasons for abortion always being wrong in Topic 2.6. The arguments against could be the Muslim arguments for abortion being allowed in certain circumstances and the Christian arguments for abortion being allowed in certain circumstances in Topic 2.6.

Topic 2.7.2 Judaism and abortion

There are different attitudes to abortion in Judaism.

1 Some Jews believe that abortion can never be allowed whatever the circumstances. They have this attitude because:
   - They believe that life begins at conception and so abortion is murder, which is banned by the sixth commandment.
   - They believe in the sanctity of life and so only God has the right to take life.

> *You shall not murder.*
>
> Exodus 20:13

2 Many Jews believe that abortion is wrong, but if the mother's life is at risk, then it is permissible. They have this attitude because:
   - They believe in the sanctity of life and so think abortion is wrong.
   - The Torah permits killing in self-defence, and they believe that, if the foetus is threatening the mother's life, abortion is a form of self-defence.

3 Some Jews believe that Jews can have abortions in accordance with the UK law on abortion. They have this attitude because:

The scrolls of the Torah in the Ark. What can we learn from this picture about what most Jews believe about the Torah?

   - They believe that life does not begin until the foetus can survive on its own because of the teachings of the Torah.
   - The Torah says that Jews must prevent avoidable suffering, which is what the UK law on abortion tries to do.
   - They also believe the self-defence argument for abortion.

> *See now that I myself am He! There is no god besides me. I put to death and I bring to life ...*
>
> Deuteronomy 32:39

Questions

b Do you agree with abortion? Give two reasons for your point of view. **4**

c Choose one religion other than Christianity and explain why some of the followers of that religion allow abortion and some do not. **8**

d 'No religious person should ever have an abortion.'
   i Do you agree? Give reasons for your opinion. **3**
   ii Give reasons why some people may disagree with you. **3**

Exam Tip

d Use the answering evaluation questions advice from page 9. The arguments for could be the Jewish reasons for abortion always being wrong plus the Christians reasons for abortion always being wrong in Topic 2.6. The arguments against could be the Jewish arguments for abortion being allowed in certain circumstances and the Christian arguments for abortion being allowed in certain circumstances in Topic 2.6.

SUMMARY

- Some Jews believe abortion is always wrong because life is in God's hands.
- Some Jews believe abortion can be allowed in certain circumstances because preventing suffering is taught in the Torah.

Topic 2.7.3 Hinduism and abortion

Do not have an abortion and do not keep the company of women who have. Do not keep the company of a woman who encourages or assists in abortion.

The Shikshapatri of Lord Swaminarayan

Unborn, eternal, everlasting, he (the soul), primeval: he is not slain when the body is slain. If a man knows him as indestructible, eternal, unborn, never to pass away, how and whom can he cause to be slain or slay.

Bhagavad Gita 2:20–21

There are different attitudes to abortion in Hinduism.

1 Some Hindus believe that abortion can never be allowed whatever the circumstances. They believe this because:
   • Some **Gurus** have said that all abortion is wrong.
   • They believe in the sanctity of life and that taking life gives bad karma.

2 Some Hindus believe that abortion is only permissible if the mother's life is at risk. They have this attitude because:
   • Hindu teachings on **ahimsa** state that violence should only be used as a last resort, which would be when the mother would die if an abortion was not carried out.
   • The sanctity of life means that abortion is wrong unless the foetus threatens the sanctity of the mother's life.

3 Some British Hindus believe that Hindus can have abortions in accordance with the UK law on abortion. They have this attitude because:
   • The teachings of the Gita on not being able to harm the soul are taken to mean that abortion will not affect karma.
   • They believe that life does not begin until the foetus can survive outside the womb.

Abortion is available on demand in India where about five million abortions a year are carried out (83 per cent of India's population is Hindu).

Questions

b Do you agree with abortion? Give two reasons for your point of view. **4**

c Choose one religion other than Christianity and explain why some of the followers of that religion allow abortion and some do not. **8**

d 'No religious person should ever have an abortion.'
   i Do you agree? Give reasons for your opinion. **3**
   ii Give reasons why some people may disagree with you. **3**

Exam Tip

d Use the answering evaluation questions advice from page 9. The arguments for could be the Hindu reasons for abortion always being wrong plus the Christians reasons for abortion always being wrong in Topic 2.6. The arguments against could be the Hindu arguments for abortion being allowed in certain circumstances and the Christian arguments for abortion being allowed in certain circumstances in Topic 2.6.

SUMMARY

• Some Hindus think abortion should never be allowed.

• Some Hindus think abortion can only be allowed if the mother's life is in danger.

• Some Hindus think abortion is allowed in any circumstances.

Topic 2.7.4 Sikhism and abortion

There are different attitudes to abortion in Sikhism.

1 Most Sikhs believe that abortion is wrong and can only be permitted if the mother's life is at risk, or the pregnancy is a result of rape. They have this attitude because:
   - They believe that human life begins at the moment of conception and as life is sacred it should not be taken.
   - They believe only God has the right to take life.
   - It is sometimes necessary to commit 'the lesser of two evils', for example, if a woman is pregnant through rape (a greater evil) or having the child will cause her death (a greater evil).

2 Some Sikhs believe that abortion is also permissible if the health of the baby or the mother are at risk,
andso they would accept the UK law on abortion.
They have this attitude because:
   - Sikhs regard each individual as important and a part of God's essence, therefore the mother is more important than the child.
   - They believe that sanctity of life involves more than just the baby (it involves the lives of the parents and siblings as well) and is also connected with the removal of suffering (babies that would suffer greatly if born).

> *A child is born when it pleases God.*
>
> **Guru Granth Sahib 921**

> *Cursed is he who kills a daughter.*
>
> **Guru Granth Sahib 1413**

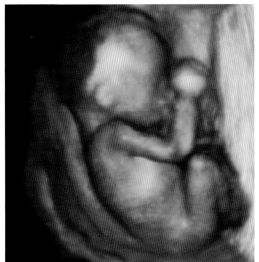

Killing girl children was condemned by the Ten Gurus. Many modern Sikhs use this teaching to condemn those who have an abortion when scans show the foetus is female.

Questions

b Do you agree with abortion? Give two reasons for your point of view. **4**

c Choose one religion other than Christianity and explain why some of the followers of that religion allow abortion and some do not. **8**

d 'No religious person should ever have an abortion.'
   i Do you agree? Give reasons for your opinion. **3**
   ii Give reasons why some people may disagree with you. **3**

Exam Tip

d Use the answering evaluation questions advice from page 9. The arguments for could be the Sikh reasons for abortion always being wrong plus the Christians reasons for abortion always being wrong in Topic 2.6. The arguments against could be the Sikh arguments for abortion being allowed in certain circumstances and the Christian arguments for abortion being allowed in certain circumstances in Topic 2.6.

SUMMARY

- Many Sikhs believe abortion is wrong except for when the mother's life is at risk or she has been raped.
- Some Sikhs believe in the UK law on abortion because they believe sanctity of life involves removing suffering.

Topic 2.8 The nature of euthanasia

KEY WORDS

Assisted suicide – providing a seriously ill person with the means to commit suicide.

Euthanasia – the painless killing of someone dying from a painful disease.

Non-voluntary euthanasia – ending someone's life painlessly when they are unable to ask, but you have good reason for thinking they would want you to do so.

Quality of life – the idea that life must have some benefits for it to be worth living.

Voluntary euthanasia – ending life painlessly when someone in great pain asks for death.

Euthanasia is normally thought of as providing a gentle and easy death to someone suffering from a painful, terminal disease who has little **quality of life**. This can be done by: **assisted suicide, voluntary euthanasia, non-voluntary euthanasia**.

British law says that all these methods of euthanasia can lead to a charge of murder. However, the law now agrees that withdrawing artificial nutrition and hydration is not murder. In the same way, withholding treatment from patients with little or no chance of survival and ensuring a peaceful death for them is not murder. These two types of euthanasia (the withdrawal or withholding of treatment) are often called passive euthanasia, in contrast to positive euthanasia which is actually bringing someone's life to an end.

Why euthanasia is a controversial issue

1 Many people want euthanasia to remain illegal because:
 • There is always likely to be doubt as to whether it is what the person really wants. If there is money involved, unscrupulous relatives might request euthanasia for a rich relative in order to gain from their will.
 • There is also the problem as to whether the disease is terminal. A cure might be found for the disease, or the patient may go into remission.
 • Doctors would also face a big problem if they started to kill patients, even though the patient requested it. It is the role of doctors to save lives, not end them. Would patients trust their doctors if they weren't sure about their dedication to saving life?
 • People might change their mind about wanting euthanasia, but then it would be too late.
 • Who would decide to allow the euthanasia to take place? What safeguards could there be that they were only killing people who really wanted and needed euthanasia?

2 Many people want euthanasia to be made legal because:
 • Advances in medicine have led to people being kept alive who would previously have died, but their quality of life is appalling. It is claimed that doctors and relatives should have the right to give such patients a painless death.

- The development of life-support machines has already brought in a form of euthanasia as doctors and relatives can agree to switch off such machines if there is no chance of the patient regaining consciousness. It is claimed that the National Health Service cannot afford to keep people alive for years on a life-support machine that could be used to save the life of someone who has a chance of recovery.
- Just as doctors can now switch off life support machines, so judges have said that doctors can stop treatment.
- Many people feel that it is a basic human right to have control about ending your life. If people have the right to commit suicide, then they have the right to ask a doctor to assist their suicide if they are too weak to do it themselves.

Nancy Crick was assisted to commit suicide by right-to-die campaigners because she had terminal cancer. After her death it was discovered that she was in remission. Her relatives and the campaigners still believe it was right. Her son said, 'It makes little difference whether she had cancer or not. Our main concern is that our mother is at peace.'

Questions

b Do you agree with euthanasia? Give two reasons for your point of view. **4**

c Explain why euthanasia is a controversial issue. **8**

d 'The law on euthanasia should be changed.'
  i Do you agree? Give reasons for your opinion. **3**
  ii Give reasons why some people may disagree with you. **3**

Exam Tip

b You should already have thought about this, and you just have to give two reasons for your opinion. For example, if you don't agree with euthanasia, you could use the reasons of unscrupulous relatives and doctors having a duty to save lives, not kill.

SUMMARY

There are various types of euthanasia that are all aimed at giving an easy death to those suffering intolerably.

British law says that euthanasia is a crime, but withholding treatment to dying patients is not.

Topic 2.9 Christian attitudes to euthanasia

Although all Christians believe that euthanasia is basically wrong, there are slightly different attitudes to the complex issues.

The use of painkillers to alleviate the suffering of the dying, even at the risk of shortening their days, can be morally in conformity with human dignity if death is not willed either as an end or a means, but only foreseen and tolerated as inevitable.

Catechism of the Catholic Church 2279

If we live, we live to the Lord; and if we die, we die to the Lord. So, whether we live or die, we belong to the Lord.

Romans 14:8

Discontinuing medical procedures that are burdensome, dangerous, extraordinary, or disproportionate to the expected outcome can be legitimate; it is the refusal of 'over-zealous' treatment.

Catechism of the Catholic Church 2278

1 Catholics and many Liberal Protestants believe that assisted suicide, voluntary euthanasia and non-voluntary euthanasia are all wrong. However, they accept that modern medicine has introduced new issues. They believe that the switching off of life-support machines is not euthanasia if brain death has been established by medical experts. They also believe that it is not wrong to allow death to occur by not giving extraordinary treatment (treatment that could cause distress to the patient and family and is only likely to put off death for a short time), nor is it wrong to give dying people painkillers which may shorten their life. They have this attitude because:

- They believe in the sanctity of life. Life is created by God and so it is sacred to God. It is up to God, not humans, when people die. Euthanasia is to put oneself on a par with God, which is condemned in the Bible.
- They regard any form of euthanasia as a form of murder, and murder is forbidden in the Ten Commandments.
- They believe that it is up to medical experts to determine when death has occurred. If doctors say someone is brain-dead, then they have already died, so switching off the machine is accepting what God has already decided and is not euthanasia.
- If you give painkillers to a dying person in great pain, and they actually kill the person, this is not wrong because your intention was to remove their pain and not to kill them (doctrine of double effect).
- Not giving extraordinary treatment is permitted by the Catechism – see Catechism 2278 quote on the left.

2 Some Christians believe any form of euthanasia is wrong and they do not allow the switching off of life-support machines, the refusal of extraordinary treatment, or the giving of large doses of painkillers. They have this attitude because:

- They take the Bible teachings literally and the Bible bans suicide. Both assisted suicide and voluntary euthanasia are forms of suicide, so they are wrong.
- They regard switching off a life-support machine, the refusal of extraordinary treatment, or giving a large dose of painkillers, as euthanasia. Life is being ended by humans not God and this is wrong.
- They regard any form of euthanasia as murder, and murder is banned by God in the Ten Commandments.

- They believe in the sanctity of life. Life is created by God and so it is sacred to God. It is up to God, not humans, when people die. Euthanasia is to put oneself on a par with God, which is condemned in the Bible.

3 A few Christians accept a limited use of euthanasia. They agree with living wills in which people state what sort of treatment they wish to receive and how they want to die if they have a terminal illness. They believe this because:
- Modern medical science means that we can no longer be sure what God's wishes about someone's death actually are.
- The teaching of Jesus on loving your neighbour and helping people in trouble could be used to justify assisting suicide.
- Living wills give people a chance to be in control of what doctors are doing to them, which is a basic human right.

The common experience of Christians throughout the ages has been that the grace of God sustains heart and mind to the end. To many, the end of life is clouded by pain and impaired judgement, and whilst we believe that it is right to use all and any medical treatment to control pain, experience denies the rightness of legalising the termination of life by a doctor, authorised by a statement signed by the patient whilst in health. Such euthanasia threatens to debase the function of doctors and impairs the confidence of their patients.

Statement by the Salvation Army in *What the Churches Say on Moral Issues*

Many Christians help in the running of hospices to ease the suffering and death of the terminally ill without euthanasia.

Questions

b Do you think switching off a life-support machine is euthanasia? Give two reasons for your point of view. **4**

c Explain two different Christian attitudes to euthanasia. **8**

d 'Life belongs to God and should only be taken by God.'
   i Do you agree? Give reasons for your opinion. **3**
   ii Give reasons why some people may disagree with you. **3**

Exam Tip

d Use the answering evaluation questions advice from page 9. The arguments for could come from the Christian arguments against euthanasia. The arguments against could be from Topic 2.8 reasons for allowing euthanasia.

SUMMARY

All Christians are against euthanasia because they believe life is sacred and belongs to God.

However, there are some different attitudes among Christians about switching off life-support machines, withdrawing treatment, and so on, because some think these are not euthanasia.

Topic 2.10.1 Islam and euthanasia

The Prophet said, 'In the time before you, a man was wounded. His wounds troubled him so much that he took a knife and cut his wrist to bleed himself to death.' Thereupon Allah said, 'My slave hurried in the matter of his life, therefore he is deprived of the Garden.'

Hadith reported in al'Burkhari

Nor can a soul die except by God's leave, the term being fixed as by writing.

Surah 3:145

All Muslims are against euthanasia, but there are two slightly different attitudes.

1   Most Muslims are against euthanasia in any form at all. They have this attitude because:
   - The Qur'an says that suicide is wrong and will result in being sent to hell on the Last Day. If suicide is wrong, then assisted suicide must also be wrong.
   - Many Muslims believe that voluntary euthanasia is just the same as assisted suicide – asking someone to kill you is no different from killing yourself, therefore it is wrong for Muslims.
   - Muslims believe in the sanctity of life so taking life by euthanasia would be murder, which is banned by the Qur'an.
   - The Qur'an says that only God has the right to give and take life, so euthanasia is putting yourself on a par with God, which could be the greatest sin of **shirk**.
   - Islam teaches that life is a test set by God and Muhammad said that ending life early (which euthanasia is) would be like cheating in the test and would lead to being sent to hell on the Last Day.

2   Some Muslims would agree with all the above points, but would feel that switching off life-support machines is not euthanasia. They have this attitude because:
   - Some Muslim lawyers have agreed that life-support machines can be switched off if doctors agree the life has ended.
   - They believe that if someone is brain-dead, God has already taken their life and so switching off the machine would not be euthanasia.

SUMMARY

All Muslims are against euthanasia because they believe life is sacred and belongs to God. However, there are some different attitudes among Muslims about the switching off of life-support machines, withdrawing treatment, and so on, because some think these are not euthanasia.

Questions

b   Do you think suicide is always wrong? Give two reasons for your point of view.   **4**

c   Choose one religion other than Christianity and explain why most of the followers of that religion are against euthanasia.   **8**

d   'Euthanasia is always wrong.'
   i   Do you agree? Give reasons for your opinion.   **3**
   ii Give reasons why some people may disagree with you.   **3**

Exam Tip

c   'Explain why' means you should use four reasons why Muslims are against euthanasia, and make each of them into a short paragraph. For tips on Quality of Written Communication, look at page 3.

Topic 2.10.2 Judaism and euthanasia

Judaism is against euthanasia, but there are two slightly different attitudes among Jewish people.

1 Most Jewish people are against euthanasia in any form at all. They have this attitude because:
  - The Torah says that suicide is wrong and will be punished by God. If suicide is wrong, then assisted suicide must also be wrong.
  - Many Jewish people believe that voluntary euthanasia is just the same as assisted suicide – asking someone to kill you is no different from killing yourself, therefore it is wrong for Jewish people.
  - Jewish people believe in the sanctity of life so taking life by euthanasia would be murder, which is banned by the **Ten Commandments**.
  - The Tenakh and the Talmud say that only God has the right to give and take life, so euthanasia is putting yourself on a par with God.

2 Some Jewish people believe that, although euthanasia is wrong, switching off life-support machines and not striving to keep someone alive are permitted. They have this attitude because:
  - Some rabbis have agreed that life-support machines can be switched off if doctors agree the life has ended.
  - They believe that if someone is brain-dead, God has already taken their life and so switching off the machine would not be euthanasia.
  - They believe that striving to keep someone alive is preventing God from taking their soul and so is against God's wishes.

> *Naked I came from my mother's womb, and naked I shall depart. The Lord gave and the Lord has taken away; may the name of the Lord be praised.*
>
> **Job 1:21**

> *If there is anything which causes a hindrance to the departure of the soul ... then it is permissible to remove it.*
>
> **Rabbi Moses Isserles**

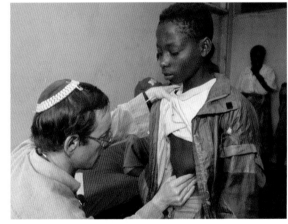

What do you think the attitude of this Jewish doctor might be to euthanasia and switching off life-support machines?

Questions

b Do you think suicide is always wrong? Give two reasons for your point of view. **4**

c Choose one religion other than Christianity and explain why most of the followers of that religion are against euthanasia. **8**

d 'Euthanasia is always wrong.'
  i Do you agree? Give reasons for your opinion. **3**
  ii Give reasons why some people may disagree with you. **3**

Exam Tip

c 'Explain why' means you should use four reasons why Jewish people are against euthanasia, and make each of them into a short paragraph. For tips on Quality of Written Communication, look at page 3.

SUMMARY

Judaism is against euthanasia because it teaches that life is sacred and belongs to God. However, there are some different attitudes among Jewish people about switching off life-support machines, withdrawing treatment, and so on, because some think these are not euthanasia.

Topic 2.10.3 Hinduism and euthanasia

Radha being persuaded to meet Lord Krishna. Does the teaching of Lord Krishna in the Gita, that killing the body cannot harm the soul, justify euthanasia?

Non-violence is the highest ethical code of behaviour. It includes non-killing, non-injury and non-harming. Do not kill any living creature ... Do not kill a human being ... Do not commit suicide.

Shikshapatri of Lord Swaminarayan

Unborn, eternal, everlasting he (the soul) primeval: he is not slain when the body is slain.

Bhagavad Gita 2:20

SUMMARY

- Some Hindus agree with euthanasia if the dying person wants to die easily because it releases the soul.
- Other Hindus only allow life-support machines to be switched off and no other form of euthanasia because life is sacred.

There are different attitudes to euthanasia in Hinduism.

1 Most Hindus are against euthanasia in any form at all. They have this attitude because:
- The teaching on ahimsa means that any harm done to humans is wrong and creates bad karma preventing moksha. So all forms of euthanasia are wrong for Hindus.
- Hindu teaching on the sanctity of life means that euthanasia would be damaging a soul, which is part of Brahman.
- The law of karma means that only God can give and take life at the right time. Euthanasia would be interfering with the law of karma and simply mean that the person would have to go through the same suffering in their next life.
- The **Laws of Manu** say that murder is wrong, and many Hindus regard euthanasia as a form of murder.
- They believe that to practise euthanasia is to put oneself on a par with God, which would create a massive amount of bad karma for the soul of the person committing it.

2 Some Hindus believe that euthanasia can be allowed in certain circumstances. Not only switching off life-support machines and not striving to keep someone alive are permitted, but also when there is no quality of life. They have this attitude because:
- They believe that if someone is brain-dead, God has already taken their life and so switching off the machine would not be euthanasia.
- They believe that striving to keep someone alive is preventing God from taking their soul and so is preventing the law of karma.
- They believe that denying death when there is no quality of life could be a form of ahimsa.
- They believe the teachings of the Gita that the soul cannot be harmed.

Questions

b Do you think suicide is always wrong? Give two reasons for your point of view. **4**

c Choose one religion other than Christianity and explain why most of the followers of that religion are against euthanasia. **8**

d 'Euthanasia is always wrong.'
  i Do you agree? Give reasons for your opinion. **3**
  ii Give reasons why some people may disagree with you. **3**

Exam Tip

c 'Explain why' means you should use four reasons why some Hindus are against euthanasia, and make each of them into a short paragraph. For tips on Quality of Written Communication, look at page 3.

Topic 2.10.4 Sikhism and euthanasia

Sikhism is against euthanasia, but there are two slightly different attitudes among Sikh people.

1 Most Sikhs are against euthanasia in any form at all. They have this attitude because:
   - Sikh teaching on violence means that any harm done to humans is wrong and creates bad **karma**, preventing mukti. So all forms of euthanasia are wrong for Sikhs.
   - Sikh teaching on the sanctity of life means that euthanasia would be damaging a soul, which is condemned in the Guru Granth Sahib.
   - Sikhism teaches that only God can give and take life at the right time. Euthanasia would be interfering with the **law of karma** and prevent both the dying person and the one who gives euthanasia from gaining mukti.
   - The **Rahit Maryada** says that murder is wrong, and many Sikhs regard euthanasia as a form of murder.
   - They believe that to practise euthanasia is to put oneself on a par with God, which is the ultimate form of manmukh and would create a massive amount of bad karma for the soul of the person committing it.

2 Many Sikhs living in Britain tend to accept British practices in such things. So, although they are against euthanasia in general, they accept that life-support machines can be switched off if a person is brain-dead. They would also accept that doctors should not strive to keep terminally ill patients alive. They have this attitude because:
   - They believe that if someone is brain-dead, God has already taken their life and so switching off the machine would not be euthanasia.
   - They believe that striving to keep someone alive is preventing God from taking their soul and so is preventing the law of karma.
   - They believe that as the aim of life is the release of the soul, people should not be kept alive artificially.

> *God sends us and we take birth. God calls us back and we die.*
>
> **Guru Granth Sahib 1239**

> *The dawn of a new day is the herald of a sunset. Earth is not your permanent home.*
>
> **Guru Granth Sahib 793**

SUMMARY

- Most Sikhs are against euthanasia because they believe life and death should be in the hands of God, and that killing brings bad karma and so will prevent mukti.
- Some Sikhs accept not striving to keep someone alive and switching off life-support machines because not to do so would prevent the release of the soul.

Questions

b Do you think suicide is always wrong? Give two reasons for your point of view. **4**

c Choose one religion other than Christianity and explain why most of the followers of that religion are against euthanasia. **8**

d 'Euthanasia is always wrong.'
   i   Do you agree? Give reasons for your opinion. **3**
   ii Give reasons why some people may disagree with you. **3**

Exam Tip

c 'Explain why' means you should use four reasons why most Sikhs are against euthanasia, and make each of them into a short paragraph. For tips on Quality of Written Communication, look at page 3.

Topic 2.11 The media and matters of life and death

Forms of communication.

The media are all forms of communication, whether written, spoken or printed. In this specification, it refers to newspapers, television, radio, films and the internet. Note that the word is plural, in the singular it would be medium.

Religion makes many statements in the media about such matters of life and death as abortion, euthanasia, transplants, genetic engineering, cloning and fertility treatments.

What you need to know about how to answer questions on this topic are:

1 arguments which say that the media should not be free to criticise what religion says about these issues

2 arguments which say that the media must be allowed to criticise what religion says about these issues.

1. Arguments that the media should not be free to criticise what religions say about matters of life and death

- Some people would argue that criticising what religions say about issues like abortion and genetic engineering is a way of stirring up religious hatred, which is banned by the Racial and Religious Hatred Act of 2007.

  For example, the Catholic Church told Catholics to withdraw their support from Amnesty International because Amnesty had decided in 2007 to back abortion as a human right for women who had been raped. When the media reported this, they quoted examples that were bound to show the Catholic position in a bad light. One of the examples used related to the Christian women of Darfur who were gang-raped by Sudanese soldiers and were expected to have the babies and bring them up, even though their husbands and families rejected them.

- Many religious believers would argue that there should be some restrictions on the freedom of the media because criticism of religious attitudes can cause serious offence to believers.

  For example, when the Danish newspaper *Jyllands-Posten* published cartoons of the Prophet Muhammad, thousands of Muslims around the world were very offended and there were riots in some countries. (See the photo on page 63.)

In 2006 a Danish newspaper printed cartoons of the Prophet Muhammad, which caused worldwide protest by Muslims who believe the prophet should not be pictured. This picture shows Pakistanis at a protest rally. Do you think that there should be total freedom of speech, or that where offence can be caused the media should exercise restraint?

- Some religious believers would argue that criticising what religious leaders such as the Pope or the Archbishop of Canterbury say about matters of life and death is close to the crime of blasphemy. Essentially, if the media criticise the Pope's teachings on a topic like abortion or euthanasia, they are condemning the Catholic Church.

  The last trial on the blasphemy law was in 1977, when the trial judge said blasphemous libel was committed if a publication about God, Christ, the Christian religion or the Bible used words that were scurrilous, abusive or offensive, which vilified Christianity and might lead to a breach of the peace.
- Some religious believers might feel that because their attitude is based on what God says, it should not be criticised because God is beyond human criticism.

It is deeply misguided to propose a law by which it would be legal for the terminally ill to be killed or assisted in suicide by those caring for them, even if there are safeguards to ensure it is only the terminally ill who would qualify. To take this step would fundamentally undermine the basis of law and medicine and undermine the duty of the state to care for vulnerable people ...
As a result many who are ill or dying would feel a burden to others. The right to die would become the duty to die.

Part of a joint submission by all the Church of England and Catholic bishops to the House of Lords Select Committee on the Assisted Dying for the Terminally Ill Bill. Should the media have a right to criticise such statements?

2. Arguments that the media should be free to criticise what religions say about matters of life and death

- All societies with democratic forms of government claim to believe in freedom of expression (it is Article 10 of the European Convention on Human Rights). In order for democracy to work, the electorate has to be able to make informed choices before they vote. For this they need a free media so that they can know what is going on in the world and in their own country and they can then work out which political party will deal best with the problems of the country and the world. If the media have freedom of expression, then they must be free to criticise religious attitudes to matters of life and death.

- Many religious leaders use the media to criticise government policies on matters of life and death, for example the use of human embryos for stem cell research. If religions wish to have the right to criticise the attitudes of other people on issues of life and death, they must be prepared to have their attitudes criticised.

- In a multi-faith society such as the United Kingdom, there must be freedom of religious belief and expression (as guaranteed by Article 9 of the European Convention on Human Rights). This means that the media must have the right to question and even criticise not only religious beliefs, but also what religions say about controversial issues such as abortion, euthanasia and genetic engineering.

- Life and death issues are of such importance to everyone that people want to know what is the right thing to do about them. Society cannot find the truth by allowing religions to put forward opinions that no one can criticise. A free media gives religious people a chance to put forward their ideas whilst at the same time allowing non-religious people (or people from a different religion) the chance to put forward their ideas.

Mongolians voting in the fifth general election since democracy was established in the 1990s. Do voters need a free press to be able to cast their votes properly?

- Sir Karl Popper, one of the greatest twentieth-century philosophers, argued that freedom of expression is essential for human societies to make progress. He claimed that it is no accident that the most advanced societies also have the greatest freedoms for their citizens. According to Popper, progress is made by subjecting all ideas, policies and so on to scrutiny, discovering what is false in them and then putting forward a new form without the false elements. This can only happen if government policies and religious attitudes can be scrutinised by a free media.

Sir Karl Popper.

Questions

b Do you think the media should be free to criticise religion? Give two reasons for your point of view. **4**

c Explain why people argue about the way the media treat religion. **8**

d 'The media should not criticise religious attitudes to abortion.'
  i Do you agree? Give reasons for your opinion. **3**
  ii Give reasons why some people may disagree with you. **3**

Exam Tip

d Use the answering evaluation questions advice from page 9. The arguments for could be three of the reasons from point 1 of this topic. Arguments against could be three of the reasons from point 2 of this topic.

SUMMARY

Some people think that what religions say about matters of life and death should not be criticised by the media because:

- They might stir up religious hatred.
- They might be offensive to religious believers.

Other people think the media should be free to criticise religious attitudes because:

- A free media is a key part of democracy.
- If religions want to be free to say what they want, then the media must also be free to criticise religion.

How to answer exam questions

Question A **What is non-voluntary euthanasia?**   2 marks

Ending someone's life painlessly when they are unable to ask, but you have good reason for thinking they would want you to do so.

Question B **Do you agree with abortion?**
Give two reasons for your point of view.   4 marks

Yes I do agree with abortion because I don't think a foetus is a human life until it is capable of living outside the mother. Therefore abortions before 24 weeks are not taking life. I also believe that a woman should have the right to do what she wants with her own body. The problems caused to a woman by having an unwanted baby justify her having an abortion.

Question C **Choose one religion other than Christianity and explain why most of its followers are against euthanasia.**   8 marks

Muslims are mainly against euthanasia because in the Qur'an it teaches that humans are one of Allah's greatest creations and so to take away Allah's creation is a sin. Muslims regard the Qur'an as the word of Allah and so they must obey what the Qur'an says.

Muslims also believe that life is a test from Allah, so if someone is terminally ill they should not be relieved of their pain as it is a test of their faith in Allah. If they stay true to Allah they will be rewarded for that with an afterlife in eternal paradise. Therefore to commit euthanasia is not necessary as people will be relieved of their suffering in Allah's own way.

Another reason is that most Muslims regard any type of euthanasia as a form of murder. As murder is totally forbidden in the Qur'an, no Muslims should commit or allow euthanasia.

Muslims also believe in the sanctity of life, that life is precious and a gift from Allah. This means that no one has the authority to take away life but Allah, as he is the one who created it, therefore euthanasia is wrong.

Question D **'Your soul will never die.'**

  i Do you agree? Give reasons for your opinion.   3 marks

  ii Give reasons why some people may disagree with you.   3 marks

i I disagree. I don't see how the soul can live on after the death of the brain. What is your soul if it is not the brain? The evidence of science is that the human mind developed as the brain grew more complex, and so the mind cannot exist without the brain (for example, people who are brain-dead on a life-support machine). Also, where would souls live after the death of the body? Space exploration has shown there is no heaven above the sky and physics has shown there is no non-material world on earth. Finally there is no evidence for souls living after death. All the evidence for the paranormal is capable of being disproven.

ii Christians might agree with this because they believe there is life after death because Jesus rose from the dead. Also it is part of the creeds to believe in the life everlasting, which means the soul cannot die. They might quote as evidence that Jesus said to one of the robbers crucified with him, 'This day you will be with me in paradise.' They take this to mean that the robber's soul would not die at the crucifixion but live on in heaven.

QUESTION A
A high mark answer because it is a correct definition of the key word.

QUESTION B
A high mark answer because an opinion is backed up by two developed reasons.

QUESTION C
A high mark answer because four reasons for Muslims being against euthanasia are developed. A formal style of English is used and there is good use of specialist vocabulary – Qur'an, Allah, creation, test of faith, eternal paradise, sanctity of life.

QUESTION D
A high mark answer because it states the candidate's own opinion and backs it up with three clear reasons for thinking that the soul will die. It then gives three reasons for people disagreeing and believing that the soul will never die.

Section 3 Marriage and the family

Introduction

This section of the examination specification requires you to look at issues surrounding sex and marriage, divorce, family life, homosexuality and contraception.

Sex and marriage

You will need to understand the effects of, and give reasons for your own opinion about:

- changing attitudes to marriage, divorce, family life and homosexuality
- attitudes to sex outside marriage in Christianity
- attitudes to sex outside marriage in one religion other than Christianity.

Divorce

You will need to understand the effects of, and give reasons for your own opinion about:

- different Christian attitudes to divorce and the reasons for them
- different attitudes to divorce in one religion other than Christianity, and the reasons for them.

Family life

You will need to understand the effects of, and give reasons for your own opinion about:

- Christian teachings on family life and its importance
- the teachings of one religion other than Christianity on family life and its importance.

Homosexuality

You will need to understand the effects of, and give reasons for your own opinion about:

- Christian attitudes to homosexuality and the reasons for them
- attitudes to homosexuality in one religion other than Christianity, and the reasons for them.

Contraception

You will need to understand the effects of, and give reasons for your own opinion about:

- different Christian attitudes to contraception and the reasons for them
- different attitudes to contraception in one religion other than Christianity, and the reasons for them.

Topic 3.1 Changing attitudes to marriage and family life

KEY WORDS

Civil partnership – a legal ceremony giving a homosexual couple the same legal rights as a husband and wife.

Cohabitation – living together without being married.

Nuclear family – mother, father and children living as a unit.

Re-constituted family – where two sets of children (step-brothers and step-sisters) become one family when their divorced parents marry each other.

The British Social Attitudes Survey 2008 revealed these facts about what people think:

66% of people think there is little difference between marriage and living together

48% think that living with a partner shows just as much commitment as marriage

72% think unmarried couples are just as good parents as married ones

78% think that conflict between parents is more harmful to children than divorce

75% think that a mother and step-father can bring up children just as well as the biological parents

In the United Kingdom in the 1960s, it was expected that: young people would not have sex until they were married; most people would be married in church by the age of 25; most marriages would last for life; most families would be husband and wife and their children (nuclear family); homosexuals would not be seen in public because homosexual sex between adult males was a criminal offence.

How attitudes have changed

- Most people now have sex before they get married.
- It is now quite acceptable for couples to live together (cohabit) rather than marry and a greater percentage are doing so. Most people who marry are now living with their partner first.
- The average age for marrying has increased enormously (31.8 for men and 29.7 for women in 2006).
- Only a minority of marriages now take place in church (60 per cent in 1970, 34 per cent in 2006).
- Divorce is accepted as a normal part of life, and no one is looked down on for being divorced. There has been a great increase in the number of divorces.
- The extended family is becoming more popular as more mothers are in paid employment and use retired grandparents to look after the children.
- Single-parent families have increased considerably as more couples divorce.
- There are far more families where the children are being brought up by cohabiting parents (11 per cent of all families in 2006).

Do you think this nuclear family would be any different if the parents were cohabiting rather than being married?

- Re-constituted families are increasing rapidly as more people divorce and remarry.
- Homosexual sex in private between two consenting adults (over 21) was made legal in 1967 and subsequent reforms have led to society treating homosexual sex the same way as heterosexual sex.

- The **Civil Partnerships** Act 2004 created a new legal relationship of civil partnership. This is where two people of the same sex can form a union or partnership by signing a registration document. It provides same-sex couples with the same rights and treatment as opposite-sex couples who enter into a civil marriage.

Reasons for the changes

Cohabitation and marriage

- The increased availability of effective contraception (especially the contraceptive pill) made it safer to have sex.
- Christianity lost its influence as fewer people went to church and so were not encouraged to refrain from sex until they married.
- There was increased media publicity of celebrities, which made cohabitation appear respectable and led to it becoming more popular.
- The presentation on television and in films of sexual relationships outside marriage as the norm led to more people regarding sex outside marriage as acceptable.

Divorce

- In 1969, new laws made divorce much cheaper and easier to obtain for ordinary people. This led to a huge increase in the number of divorces.
- Expectations of what marriage should be like have changed greatly. Increased equality for women means that women are no longer prepared to accept unequal treatment from men. Women expect to have as good a life as their husbands and if their husbands treat them badly, they will divorce them.
- Before the equal rights legislation (see page 102), married women were often dependent on their husbands for financial support. Nowadays, many women are financially independent and can afford to live after a divorce.
- Demographic changes – there has also been a great change in how long people are likely to be married. A hundred years ago, many men could expect to have more than one wife because so many women died in childbirth. Most divorces occur after ten years of marriage, which was the average length of a marriage 100 years ago.

In 2005, the government and the Church agreed to the marriage of Prince Charles to Camilla Parker Bowles, even though both had been divorced.

Most cohabiting couples think that they have the same rights about financial support, property, children, and so on, as they would if they were married, but this is not the case. 'The law that currently applies to such couples (cohabiting couples) on separation is unclear and complicated, and it can produce unfair outcomes. This causes serious hardship not only to cohabitants themselves, but also to their children.'

Statement from the Law Commission about proposals to give legal rights to cohabiting couples that were shelved in March 2008

Changing attitudes and STD
Some people think that the changing attitudes to sex and marriage have led to a large increase in sexually transmitted diseases. Cases of sexually transmitted diseases rose by 63 per cent between 1997 and 2006 and the incidence of Chlamydia (which can lead to cancer and infertility) rose 166 per cent between 1997 and 2006.

Source: National Statistics Online

SUMMARY

Fifty years ago, most people only had sex in marriage, and they married in church. Now, people have sex before they marry, cohabiting is acceptable and most marriages are not in church. This could be caused by safer contraception and fewer people being influenced by religion.

Divorce and re-marriage used to be rare but are accepted today, and two in five marriages end in divorce. The changes may have been caused by cheaper divorce and women having more equality.

Family life has changed so that, although most children are still brought up by a mother and a father, the parents may not be married or they may have been married more than once. These changes are probably caused by the changing attitudes to sex, marriage and divorce.

Homosexuality used to be illegal, but now homosexuals have the same rights to sexual activity as heterosexuals including civil partnerships. These changes are probably due to discoveries showing homosexuality is natural and changes to the law.

Family life

- The increase in the number of cohabiting couples means that there are now many more families where the parents are not married.
- The increase in divorce has led to an increase in **re-marriage** (most people who divorce before the age of 50 re-marry). This means that there are now many more re-constituted families.
- The extended family is becoming more popular as more mothers are in paid employment and use retired grandparents or non-working close relatives to look after the children.
- The increase in the number of divorces plus the acceptance by society of unmarried mothers has led to an increase in the number of single-parent families.

Homosexuality

- The various changes in the laws on **homosexuality** have made it easier to be openly homosexual and made society more aware and accepting of homosexuality.
- Medical research has shown that homosexuality is most probably genetic. As society began to realise homosexuality is therefore 'normal', so people began to accept equal status and rights for homosexual couples.
- The increased openness of gay celebrities has led to a greater acceptance of all gay people.
- The work of such organisations as Stonewall changed many people's attitudes and led to a greater acceptance of equal rights for homosexuals.

Elton John and David Furnish on the day they formed their civil partnership. Do you think civil partnerships are a good idea?

Questions

b Do you think homosexuals should be allowed to marry? Give two reasons for your point of view. **4**

c Explain why attitudes to marriage and divorce have changed. **8**

d 'There's no difference between living with a partner and being married to them.'

   i Do you agree? Give reasons for your opinion. **3**

   ii Give reasons why some people may disagree with you. **3**

Exam Tip

c 'Explain' means give reasons. To answer this question you should use two reasons from cohabitation and marriage and two from divorce, and make each of them into a short paragraph. For tips on Quality of Written Communication, look at page 3.

Topic 3.2 Christian attitudes to sex outside marriage

Christianity teaches that sex should only take place between a man and woman married to each other. Therefore most Christians believe that sex outside marriage is wrong because:

- Christianity teaches that sex was given to humans by God for the procreation of children and children should be brought up in a Christian family so sex should only take place within marriage.
- The Bible says that fornication (a word used in religion for both pre-marital sex and promiscuity) is sinful and Christians should follow the teachings of the Bible.
- The Catechism of the Catholic Church teaches that pre-marital sex is wrong and Catholics should follow the teachings of the Catechism.
- All Christians are against adultery because it breaks the wedding vows to be faithful to each other.
- They are also against adultery because it is condemned in the Ten Commandments, which all Christians should follow.
- Adultery is condemned by Jesus in the Gospels and all Christians should follow the teachings of Jesus.

Some Christians accept that couples may live together before marriage, but they would expect them to marry when starting a family and would only accept a sexual relationship between two people committed to a long-term relationship.

> *The sexual act must always take place exclusively within marriage ... Human love does not tolerate 'trial marriages'. It demands a total and definitive gift of persons to one another.*
>
> **Catechism of the Catholic Church 2390–91**

> *Cohabiting couples should be welcomed and supported by the Church, 'recognising that for many this is a step along the way to the fuller commitment of marriage'.*
>
> ***Something to Celebrate***
> **A report published by the Church of England's Board of Responsibility in 1995**

KEY WORDS

Adultery – a sexual act between a married person and someone other than their marriage partner.

Faithfulness – staying with your marriage partner and having sex only with them.

Pre-marital sex – sex before marriage.

Procreation – making a new life.

Promiscuity – having sex with a number of partners without commitment.

SUMMARY

- All Christians believe adultery is wrong as it breaks one of the Ten Commandments.
- Most Christians believe that sex before marriage is wrong because the Church and the Bible teach this.

Exam Tip

c 'Explain' means give reasons. To answer this question you should use two reasons against pre-marital sex and two reasons against adultery, and make each of them into a short paragraph. For tips on Quality of Written Communication, look at page 3.

Questions

b Do you think Christians should be allowed to have sex before marriage? Give two reasons for your point of view. **4**

c Explain why most Christians are against sex outside marriage. **8**

d 'Christians should never have sex outside marriage.'
   i Do you agree? Give reasons for your opinion. **3**
   ii Give reasons why some people may disagree with you. **3**

Topic 3.3.1 Islam and sex outside marriage

Because Islam emphasises chastity and modesty, there is normally very little contact between young Muslim men and women ... there is no such thing as dating or pre-marital intimacy of any kind. In Islam, sexual behaviour and acts are only for those legally married.

From *What Does Islam Say?*, I. Hewitt

The woman and the man guilty of adultery and fornication, flog each of them with a hundred stripes: let not compassion move you in a matter prescribed by God.

Surah 24:2

SUMMARY

Muslims believe that sex before marriage and adultery are both wrong because the Qur'an teaches this.

Islam teaches that sex should only take place between a man and woman married to each other. Therefore Muslims believe that sex outside marriage is wrong because:

- Sex before marriage is forbidden by the Qur'an, which also states that boys and girls should be separated after puberty. Muslims believe the Qur'an is the word of God.
- The Shari'ah says that sex should only take place in marriage and the Shari'ah is the law for all Muslims.
- Islam teaches that the primary purpose of sex is for the procreation of children and children should only be born in a family where the mother and father are married.
- Adultery is condemned by God in the Qur'an, which says anyone committing adultery should be punished severely.
- Adultery breaks the marriage contract that both husband and wife agreed to of their own free will.
- Adultery is likely to harm the family. Both the Qur'an and Shari'ah teach that nothing should be done to harm the family, and so adultery must be avoided.

Young people holding hands. Why do you think some Muslim parents would forbid this?

Questions

b Do you think sex before marriage is wrong? Give two reasons for your point of view. **4**

c Choose one religion other than Christianity and explain why its followers are against sex outside marriage. **8**

d 'No religious person should ever have sex outside marriage.'
  i Do you agree? Give reasons for your opinion. **3**
  ii Give reasons why some people may disagree with you. **3**

Exam Tip

c 'Explain' means give reasons. To answer this question you should use two reasons against pre-marital sex and two reasons against adultery, and make each of them into a short paragraph. For tips on Quality of Written Communication, look at page 3.

Topic 3.3.2 Judaism and sex outside marriage

Judaism teaches that sex should only take place between a man and woman married to each other. Therefore Jewish people believe that sex outside marriage is wrong because:

- Fornication is forbidden by the Torah, which all Jewish people should follow. Fornication means pre-marital sex and so Jewish people should avoid sex before marriage.
- The Talmud says that sex should only take place in marriage and as the Talmud is the authorised commentary on the mitzvot, Jewish people should avoid sex outside marriage.
- Judaism teaches that the primary purpose of sex is for the procreation of children and children should only be born in a family where the mother and father are married. Therefore there should be no sex before marriage.
- Adultery is wrong because it is condemned by God in the Ten Commandments, which all Jewish people should follow.
- Adultery breaks the marriage contract that both husband and wife agreed to of their own free will.
- Adultery is likely to harm the family, which is the basis of Judaism. Children are the future of Judaism and the family is where the children learn about Judaism and how to live the Jewish life, so nothing should be done that might harm the family.

Some **Progressive Jews** do not condemn cohabitation before marriage as long as the couple are committed to each other, restrict sex to each other and intend to marry in the future.

> *The Torah lists the forbidden sexual relationships and then says, 'You shall be Holy' (Leviticus 19:2). This tells you that even in a permitted relationship, you must sanctify yourself (keep yourself holy).*
>
> **Rabbi Moses ben Nachman 1194–1270**

> *Judaism teaches that sexuality plays an important role in human relationships. However, it also recognises that the sexual urge can generate very powerful emotions, and that for this reason sexual behaviour must be carefully regulated.*
>
> **From *Moral Issues in Judaism***

A Jewish school for boys. Why do you think there are no girls at this school?

Questions

b Do you think sex before marriage is wrong? Give two reasons for your point of view. **4**

c Choose one religion other than Christianity and explain why its followers are against sex outside marriage. **8**

d 'No religious person should ever have sex outside marriage.'
   i Do you agree? Give reasons for your opinion. **3**
   ii Give reasons why some people may disagree with you. **3**

Exam Tip

c 'Explain' means give reasons. To answer this question you should use two reasons against pre-marital sex and two reasons against adultery, and make each of them into a short paragraph. For tips on Quality of Written Communication, look at page 3.

SUMMARY

- All Jews believe adultery is wrong as it breaks one of the Ten Commandments.
- Most Jews believe that sex before marriage is wrong because the Torah teaches this.
- Some Jews believe that sex before marriage can be accepted with certain conditions.

Topic 3.3.3 Hinduism and sex outside marriage

Hinduism emphasises the positive value of human sexuality, and by depicting ideal relationships (for example between Krishna and Radha, or between Rama and Sita) it offers an image of religious devotion and examples for people to follow.

From *Guidelines for Life* by Mel Thompson

O married men and women; be loving and faithful to one another.

Shikshapatri of Lord Swaminarayan

Hinduism teaches that sex should only take place between a man and woman married to each other. Therefore Hindus believe that sex outside marriage is wrong because:

- Before marriage, a Hindu is in the student stage of life (ashrama) where sex is not allowed. Therefore sex before marriage is breaking one's dharma and will prevent one from gaining moksha.
- The Hindu scriptures say that sex should only take place in marriage, and Hindus should follow the guidance of the scriptures.
- Hinduism teaches that the primary purpose of sex is for the procreation of children and children should only be born in a family where the mother and father are married. Therefore there should be no sex before marriage.
- Adultery is banned in the householder stage of life (ashrama). Therefore committing adultery is betraying one's dharma, which prevents a soul from achieving moksha.
- Adultery is a betrayal of the marriage partner and betrayal brings bad karma, which also prevents a soul from gaining moksha.
- Hinduism teaches that the family is very important as it is where children learn to be good Hindus. Also the marriage will have united two families who will both be hurt by adultery.

SUMMARY

Hindus believe that sex before marriage and adultery are both wrong because sex is only allowed in the householder stage of life and adultery brings bad karma.

Rama and Sita are regarded as an ideal Hindu married couple who were faithful to each other.

Questions

b Do you think sex before marriage is wrong? Give two reasons for your point of view. **4**

c Choose one religion other than Christianity and explain why its followers are against sex outside marriage. **8**

d 'No religious person should ever have sex outside marriage.'

   i Do you agree? Give reasons for your opinion. **3**

   ii Give reasons why some people may disagree with you. **3**

Exam Tip

c 'Explain' means give reasons. To answer this question you should use two reasons against pre-marital sex and two reasons against adultery, and make each of them into a short paragraph. For tips on Quality of Written Communication, look at page 3.

Topic 3.3.4 Sikhism and sex outside marriage

Sikhism teaches that sex should only take place between a man and woman married to each other. Therefore Sikhs believe that sex outside marriage is wrong because:

- The Gurus all restricted sex to marriage. All Sikhs should follow the example of the human Gurus and so should not have sex before marriage.

> *The Beloved (God) has completed the union. The bride's mind has blossomed with the Beloved's name.*
>
> **Lavan wedding hymn**

- The Rahit Maryada says there should be no sex before marriage. The Rahit Maryada relates the teachings of the Guru Granth Sahib to modern life and so Sikhs should follow its teachings.
- The family is the centre of Sikhism and marriages are usually arranged by families. Having sex before marriage would make this more difficult.
- Adultery is breaking the marriage union. A Sikh marriage should make a husband and wife one. Breaking the union would be manmukh behaviour which would make attaining mukti more difficult.
- Adultery is forbidden by the Rahit Maryada. As all good Sikhs should follow the advice of the Rahit Maryada, no good Sikh should commit adultery.
- All the human Gurus were faithful husbands who never committed adultery, and it is the duty of all Sikhs to follow the examples of the human Gurus.
- Sikhism teaches that the family is very important as it is where children learn to be good Sikhs. Also the marriage will have united two families who will both be hurt by adultery.

Guru Gobind Singh with his wife. Why should Sikhs follow the example of the Gurus?

> *The Rahit Maryada says, 'A Sikh should respect another man's wife as he would his own mother, and another man's daughter as his own daughter.'*

> *The bride should know no other man except her husband, so the Guru ordains … Another person's property, another man's wife, talking ill of another, poisons one's life. Like the touch of a poisonous snake is the touch of another man's wife.*
>
> **Advice on marriage from Guru Amar Das from the Sikh Marriage ceremony**

Questions

b Do you think sex before marriage is wrong? Give two reasons for your point of view. **4**

c Choose one religion other than Christianity and explain why its followers are against sex outside marriage. **8**

d 'No religious person should ever have sex outside marriage.'
   i Do you agree? Give reasons for your opinion. **3**
   ii Give reasons why some people may disagree with you. **3**

Exam Tip

c 'Explain' means give reasons. To answer this question you should use two reasons against pre-marital sex and two reasons against adultery, and make each of them into a short paragraph. For tips on Quality of Written Communication, look at page 3.

SUMMARY

Sikhs believe that sex outside marriage is wrong. Sex before marriage is banned by the Rahit Maryada. Adultery breaks the sacred marriage union.

Topic 3.4 Christian attitudes to divorce

Thus the marriage bond has been established by God himself in such a way that a marriage concluded and consummated between baptised persons can never be dissolved.

Catechism of the Catholic Church 1640

The re-marriage of persons divorced from a living, lawful spouse contravenes the plan and law of God as taught by Christ.

Catechism of the Catholic Church 1665

*For those who have taken their vows before God as Christians, there is no divorce. But most **Baptists** would acknowledge that human beings can make mistakes, and what appeared as a life-long relationship may eventually break down.*

Statement by the Baptist Church in *What the Churches Say on Moral Issues*

There are different attitudes to divorce in Christianity:

1 The Catholic Church does not allow religious divorce or **re-marriage**. Catholic marriage is a sacrament and the exchange of vows means that the only way a marriage between baptised Catholics can be dissolved (which is what divorce means) is by the death of one of the partners.

However, the Catholic Church does allow for the legal separation of spouses if they find it impossible to live together, and even civil divorce (an ending of the marriage according to the laws of the country but not the Church) if that will ensure the proper care of the children. Neither of these routes, however, has ended the marriage: the couple are still married in the eyes of God and the Church and so cannot re-marry. Catholics have this attitude because:

- Jesus taught that divorce is wrong in Mark's Gospel and Christians should follow the teachings of Jesus.
- The couple have made a **covenant** with God in the sacrament of marriage and that covenant cannot be broken by any earthly power.
- The Church teaches very clearly in the Catechism that a marriage cannot be dissolved and so religious divorce is impossible. Catholics should follow the teachings of the Church and so should not divorce.
- As there can be no religious divorce, there can be no re-marriage because that would be the same as bigamy and adultery, both of which are very serious sins.

Why do you think divorce is sometimes considered the lesser of two evils?

However, the Catholic Church does allow annulment (a declaration that the marriage was never a true marriage and so the partners are free to marry) if it can be proved that the marriage was never a true Christian marriage.

2 Most non-Catholic Churches think that divorce is wrong, but allow it if the marriage has broken down. Most of these Churches allow divorced people to remarry, but they usually require them to talk to the priest/minister about why their first marriages failed. They are sometimes asked to show repentance for the failure and required to promise that this time their marriage will be for life.

Non-Catholic Churches allow divorce because:
- Jesus allowed divorce in Matthew 19:9 for a partner's adultery, therefore Jesus showed that divorce can happen if the reasons for it are sufficiently severe.
- They believe that there are certain situations where Christians must choose 'the lesser of two evils'. If a marriage has really broken down then the effects of the couple not divorcing would be a greater evil than the evil of divorce itself.
- Christians are allowed forgiveness and a new chance if they confess their sins and are truly repentant. This belief in forgiveness should apply to divorce and re-marriage as much as anything else. So a couple should have another chance at marriage as long as they are determined to make it work the second time.
- It is the teaching of these Churches that it is better to divorce than live in hatred and quarrel all the time.

What type of Christian do you think might have drawn this cartoon?

Where a local church is in touch with one or both of the parties to a failed marriage, the offer of new life and the healing of memories is to be made. The possibility of new relationships and, where appropriate, a new marriage, is to be welcomed.

Statement by the Methodist Church in *What the Churches Say on Moral Issues*

When they were in the house again, the disciples asked Jesus about this. He answered 'Anyone who divorces his wife and marries another woman commits adultery against her. And if she divorces her husband and marries another man, she commits adultery.'

Mark 10:10–12

I tell you that anyone who divorces his wife, except for marital unfaithfulness, and marries another woman commits adultery.

Matthew 19:9

Questions
b Do you think divorce is better than an unhappy marriage? Give two reasons for your point of view. **4**
c Explain why some Christians allow divorce and some do not. **8**
d 'No Christian should ever get divorced.'
  i Do you agree? Give reasons for your opinion. **3**
  ii Give reasons why some people may disagree with you. **3**

Exam Tip
b You should already have thought about this, and you just have to give two reasons for your opinion. For example, if you agree with divorce you could use two reasons for non-Catholic Churches agreeing with divorce.

SUMMARY
- Catholics do not allow religious divorce and re-marriage because they believe the marriage vows cannot be broken.
- Other Christians disapprove of divorce, but allow religious divorce and re-marriage if the marriage has broken down because Christianity teaches forgiveness.

Topic 3.5.1 Islam and divorce

> O Prophet! When ye do divorce women, divorce them at their prescribed periods ... and fear God your Lord: and turn them not out of their houses.
>
> **Surah 65:1–2**

> Ibn Omer reported that the Messenger of Allah said, 'The most detestable of lawful things near Allah is divorce.'
>
> **Hadith recorded by Abu Daud**

> Once a divorce is irrevocable, a woman is free to re-marry whoever she wishes (as long as she and her husband-to-be follow the terms of Islamic Law) and her former husband must not do anything to prevent her from doing so.
>
> **From What does Islam say? by I. Hewitt**

SUMMARY

- Most Muslims allow divorce because it is allowed by the Qur'an.
- Some Muslims do not allow divorce because Muhammad said God disapproves of it.

Divorce and re-marriage are allowed in Islam, but there are different attitudes to it among Muslims.

1 Some Muslims think that marriage should be for life and they would not divorce because:
- Muhammad is reported to have said that divorce is the most hated of lawful things. Many Muslims regard the hadith of Muhammad as almost as important as the Qur'an and so they follow what Muhammad said.
- Most marriages are arranged by families so there is parental pressure against divorce to avoid family conflict.
- Islam teaches that on the Last Day, Muslims will be judged on how well they have treated their children. The threat of being sent to hell because divorce has harmed their children is a big incentive against divorce for Muslims.
- Some Muslims believe that the teaching of the Qur'an about families trying all they can to rescue the marriage during the three month waiting period (**iddah**) means that there should be no divorce.

2 Most Muslims believe that divorce should be allowed if the marriage cannot work because:
- The Qur'an clearly permits divorce. It sets out the terms of the iddah, custody of children and care for divorced wives and so divorce must be allowed for Muslims.
- The Shari'ah permits divorce and has many laws about how divorce and re-marriage should operate. As the Shari'ah is the holy law of Islam, divorce must be permitted for Muslims.
- Islam teaches that in some situations, Muslims must choose the lesser of two evils. They believe divorce is a lesser evil than forcing a couple to live in hatred and bitterness.
- Marriage is a contract in Islam. The contract has clauses about what is to happen if the couple divorce (for example, the husband must give his wife the money he put in trust for her – the **mahr**). Therefore divorce is allowed.

Questions

b Do you think divorce is wrong? Give two reasons for your point of view. **4**

c Choose one religion other than Christianity and explain why some of its followers allow divorce, but others are against it. **8**

d 'No religious person should ever get divorced.'
  i Do you agree? Give reasons for your opinion. **3**
  ii Give reasons why some people may disagree with you. **3**

Exam Tip

c 'Explain' means give reasons. To answer this question you should use two reasons why some Muslims are against divorce and give two reasons why some Muslims allow divorce, and make each of them into a short paragraph. For tips on Quality of Written Communication, look at page 3.

Topic 3.5.2 Judaism and divorce

There are three different attitudes to divorce among Jewish people.

1 Some Jewish people believe that divorce is wrong because:
   - The Talmud teaches that divorce is an offence to God, and, as the Talmud is a commentary on the Torah, Jewish people should therefore disapprove of divorce.
   - They believe that divorce will harm any children and as children need to be brought up as good followers of Judaism for the faith to survive, nothing should be done to harm children.
   - Some rabbis have taught that divorce is wrong because of the harm it can cause for one partner or the children.

2 Many Orthodox Jews allow divorce but believe it should be initiated by the man who must apply for a **get** (certificate of divorce) from the **Bet Din**. They have this attitude because:
   - The Torah has various statements that permit divorce, and the Torah is binding on Orthodox Jews.
   - Marriage in Judaism is a contract that can be broken in certain circumstances.
   - The halakhah says that only men can apply to the Bet Din for a get and that women cannot re-marry without a get (if they do, their children are regarded as illegitimate).

3 Most **Reform Jews** allow divorce and allow wives to apply for a get, or do not require a get at all. They have this attitude because:
   - They believe that the Torah and halakhah are not the direct word of God and should be interpreted in the light of the modern world.
   - They believe that men and women should have equal rights in religion (they have women rabbis), which means they should have equal rights in divorce.
   - They believe that in some situations, Jewish people must choose the lesser of two evils. They believe divorce is a lesser evil than forcing a couple to live in hatred and bitterness.

> *If a man divorces his first wife, even the altar of the Temple sheds tears.*
>
> **The Talmud**

> *If a man marries a woman who becomes displeasing to him because he finds something indecent about her ... he writes her a certificate of divorce ...*
>
> **Deuteronomy 24:1**

Y.Y. Lichtenstein, Dayan of Rosh Bet Din in London.

Questions

b Do you think divorce is wrong? Give two reasons for your point of view. **4**

c Choose one religion other than Christianity and explain why some of its followers allow divorce, but others are against it. **8**

d 'No religious person should ever get divorced.'
   i Do you agree? Give reasons for your opinion. **3**
   ii Give reasons why some people may disagree with you. **3**

Exam Tip

c 'Explain' means give reasons. To answer this question you should use two reasons why some Jewish people are against divorce and give two reasons why some Jewish people allow divorce, and make each of them into a short paragraph. For tips on Quality of Written Communication, look at page 3.

SUMMARY

- Some Jewish people are against divorce because of the teachings of the Talmud and rabbis.
- Orthodox Jews allow divorce, but give special rights to men in divorce because of the Torah.
- Reform Jews allow divorce, but give equal divorce rights to women because they think the Torah should be brought up to date.

Topic 3.5.3 Hinduism and divorce

The Brahmin said, 'It is written in scripture, your majesty: "Protect your wife." When the wife is protected, the offspring are protected. For one's self is born in one's offspring; and when the offspring are protected, the self is protected. So she must be protected, your majesty. If she is not protected, the various classes will become commingled, and that will cause one's previous ancestors to fall from heaven.'

Shastra 5.3.6

Swaminarayan ... men avoid conversation with widows and women outside their families. Indeed a man is not to be alone in a room with a woman other than his wife, not even with a daughter.

From *A New Face of Hinduism* by R. Williams

SUMMARY

- Some Hindus do not allow divorce because they believe marriage is for life.

- Many Hindus allow divorce especially if the couple cannot have children because they think arguing and quarrelling in a marriage will give bad karma.

Although all Hindus believe that marriage should, ideally, be for life, there are different attitudes to divorce among Hindus. All Hindus believe that divorced couples are free to re-marry.

1 Traditional Hindus believe that there should be no divorce. The only exceptions are if the couple are childless after fifteen years or if there is cruelty. They have this attitude because:
   - It is the teaching of the Laws of Manu which they still regard as the basic guide for Hindus.
   - They believe that, as marriage unites two families, divorce is likely to harm families and so should be discouraged.
   - They believe that having children is the key feature of the householder ashrama and so not having children would be grounds for divorce.
   - Violence in marriage would be against their belief in ahimsa and so would be grounds for divorce.

2 Many other Hindus believe that divorce should be allowed if a marriage has broken down. They have this attitude because:
   - They regard the Laws of Manu as out of date, and do not think they are binding on modern Hindus.
   - Some Gurus and **swamis** teach that divorce is acceptable for Hindus if the marriage has broken down.
   - They believe that if a couple live in hatred and discord they will gather bad karma, so divorce would be more likely to allow the soul to gain moksha.
   - They believe that in some situations, Hindus must choose the lesser of two evils. They believe divorce is a lesser evil than forcing a couple to live in hatred and bitterness.

Questions

b Do you think divorce is wrong? Give two reasons for your point of view. **4**

c Choose one religion other than Christianity and explain why some of its followers allow divorce, but others are against it. **8**

d 'No religious person should ever get divorced.'
   i Do you agree? Give reasons for your opinion. **3**
   ii Give reasons why some people may disagree with you. **3**

Exam Tip

c 'Explain' means give reasons. To answer this question you should use two reasons why some Hindus are against divorce and two reasons why some Hindus allow divorce, and make each of them into a short paragraph. For tips on Quality of Written Communication, look at page 3.

Topic 3.5.4 Sikhism and divorce

Although all Sikhs believe that marriage should, ideally, be for life, there are different attitudes to divorce among Sikhs.

1 Most Sikhs believe that there should be no divorce because:
   • Two souls are united in Sikh marriage, and if two bodies have become one spirit, they should not be split by divorce.
   • None of the Gurus divorced, and Sikhs should follow the example of the human Gurus, so they should not divorce.
   • The Rahit Maryada disapproves of divorce and all good Sikhs should follow the guidance of the Rahit Maryada because it is the authority on how to live a good Sikh life in the modern world.
   • As marriages tend to be arranged by parents, there are great family pressures to make the marriage succeed. Divorce would bring shame on both sets of parents.

2 Some Sikhs believe that divorce should be allowed if a marriage has broken down because:
   • Divorce is common in the Punjab if the couple cannot have children, and many Sikhs feel that it is right to follow the culture of the Punjab as this is where the Gurus lived.
   • They believe that if a couple live in hatred and discord they will gather bad karma. In such a situation, divorce would be more likely to allow the soul to gain mukti.
   • They believe that in some situations, Sikhs must choose the lesser of two evils. They believe divorce is a lesser evil than forcing a couple to live in hatred and bitterness.

> *It is not unknown for a bride who is not pregnant on her first wedding anniversary to be sent home to her parents in disgrace and for a divorce to follow. This aspect of Punjabi or Indian culture should have no place among Sikhs.*
>
> **From *Teach Yourself Sikhism* by W. Owen Cole**

Uniting two families in marriage is a big argument against divorce in Sikhism.

Questions

b Do you think divorce is wrong? Give two reasons for your point of view. **4**

c Choose one religion other than Christianity and explain why some of its followers allow divorce, but others are against it. **8**

d 'No religious person should ever get divorced.'
   i Do you agree? Give reasons for your opinion. **3**
   ii Give reasons why some people may disagree with you. **3**

Exam Tip

c 'Explain' means give reasons. To answer this question you should use two reasons why some Sikhs are against divorce and give two reasons why some Sikhs allow divorce, and make each of them into a short paragraph. For tips on Quality of Written Communication, look at page 3.

SUMMARY

• Some Sikhs believe there should be no divorce because marriage is for life and the Gurus did not divorce.

• Other Sikhs allow divorce because living in hatred will bring bad karma and prevent mukti.

Topic 3.6 Why family life is important for Christians

The family is the original cell of social life ... The family is the community in which, from childhood, one can learn moral values, begin to honour God and make good use of freedom. Family life is an initiation into life in society.

Catechism of the Catholic Church 2207

Children, obey your parents in the Lord, for this is right. "Honour your father and mother" — which is the first commandment with a promise — "that it may go well with you and that you may enjoy long life on the earth."
Fathers, do not exasperate your children; instead, bring them up in the training and instruction of the Lord.

Ephesians 6:1–4

Family life is important for Christians because:

- One of the main purposes of Christian marriage is to have children and bring them up in a secure and loving Christian environment so that they will come to love God and follow Jesus. Therefore the family is very important for Christians.
- Christianity teaches that the family was created by God as the basic unit of society and as the only place in which children should be brought up. Therefore it is the most important part of society and without the family society would collapse.
- Christian teaching on divorce makes it clear that Christian parents should stay together and bring up their children together because the family is so important.
- The family is the place where children learn the difference between right and wrong, so without the family there would be much more evil in the world.
- The family is the place where children are introduced to the faith through baptism/**dedication** and then through being taken to church for worship, Sunday school, festivals, and so on. This means that the family is very important for Christianity to continue and grow.

There is, however, a tradition dating back to Jesus, which says that there are more important things than the family for Christians. **Roman Catholic** priests, nuns and monks leave their families to serve God.

SUMMARY

Christians believe that the family is important because: it is taught in the Bible; Christian marriage services refer to bringing up a family as the main purposes of marriage; Christians believe that the family was created by God.

Questions

b Do you think families need a mother and father who are married? Give two reasons for your point of view. **4**

c Explain why family life is important for Christians. **8**

d 'Family life is more important for Christians than for non-religious people.'
  i Do you agree? Give reasons for your opinion. **3**
  ii Give reasons why some people may disagree with you. **3**

Exam Tip

c 'Explain' means give reasons. To answer this question you should use four of the above reasons for family life being important in Christianity, and make each of them into a short paragraph. For tips on Quality of Written Communication, look at page 3.

Topic 3.7.1 Islam and family life

Family life is important in Islam because:

- Islam teaches that children are a gift from God and that, on the Last Day, Muslim parents will be judged by God on how well they have brought up their children. Clearly as a Muslim's place in heaven depends on how well they look after their family, family life is very important.

> *Be careful of your duty to Allah and be fair and just to your children.*
>
> **Hadith quoted by al'Bukhari**

- The Qur'an teaches that the family was created by God as the basic unit of society and as the only place in which children should be brought up. As the Qur'an is the word of God, Muslims believe that the family must be the most important part of society and without the family society would collapse.

Why is it important for Muslim parents to send their children to madrasah?

- The Prophet Muhammad married and raised a family. As Muslims believe that Muhammad is the perfect example for them to follow, they must also marry and raise a family.
- Islam teaches that the family is the place where children learn the difference between right and wrong, so without the family there would be much more evil in the world.
- The family is the place where children are introduced to the faith through **aqiqa**, **Salah** and Ramadan at home, being taken to **madrasah**, festivals, and so on. This means that the family is very important for Islam to continue and grow.

SUMMARY

Family life is important in Islam because the Qur'an says that the family is the basis of society and Muslims should follow the example of Muhammad who raised a family.

Questions

b Do you think family life is important? Give two reasons for your point of view. **4**

c Choose one religion other than Christianity and explain why family life is important in that religion. **8**

d 'Family life is more important for religious people than for non-religious people.'
   i Do you agree? Give reasons for your opinion. **3**
   ii Give reasons why some people may disagree with you. **3**

Exam Tip

d Remember to use the techniques for answering evaluation questions on page 9. Arguments for the statement would be the reasons in this topic. Arguments against would have to come from your class discussion or your own ideas. For example, if your own family is not religious, you could give examples of how important your family is to you and your parents.

Topic 3.7.2 Judaism and family life

> *Honour your father and your mother, so that you may live long in the land the Lord your God is giving you.*
>
> Exodus 20:12

The Chief Rabbi, Jonathan Sacks, who has held parenting seminars to help Jewish parents with their family life.

> *Today, the many elements in life which once held together are splitting apart. When we create a marriage, when we bring new life into the world, when we care for it, we are carrying out supreme religious acts. But how do we do it? To this, Judaism gave a simple answer, for it is above all a practical religion. The first and most important rule is: Make time for your children.*
>
> **Jonathan Sacks, Chief Rabbi**

SUMMARY

Family life is important in Judaism because the family is the only way of keeping Judaism alive and the Torah says all Jews should marry and raise a family.

Family life is important in Judaism because:

- Judaism teaches that the family was created by God as the basic unit of society and as the only place in which children should be brought up. Therefore it is the most important part of society and without the family society would collapse.
  - It is a religious duty for Jewish people to marry and have children, indeed it is one of the mitzvot. As obeying the mitzvot is an essential part of being Jewish, so family life is an essential part of Judaism.
  - Judaism is usually passed on by birth, and only children of married Jewish parents are automatically Jewish. Therefore the family is extremely important as the way to ensure the continuation of the Jewish people and religion.
  - Judaism teaches that the family is the place where children learn the difference between right and wrong, so without the family there would be much more evil in the world.
- In Judaism, the family is the place where children are introduced to the faith through **brit milah**, observing Shabbat at home, being taken to **synagogue**, celebrating festivals, and so on. This means that the family is very important for Judaism to continue and grow.
- The Torah and halakhah outline the nature of Jewish family life and its importance is shown in the fifth of the Ten Commandments.

Questions

b Do you think family life is important? Give two reasons for your point of view. **4**

c Choose one religion other than Christianity and explain why family life is important in that religion. **8**

d 'Family life is more important for religious people than for non-religious people.'

   i Do you agree? Give reasons for your opinion. **3**

   ii Give reasons why some people may disagree with you. **3**

Exam Tip

d Remember to use the techniques for answering evaluation questions on page 9. Arguments for the statement would be the reasons in this topic. Arguments against would have to come from your class discussion or your own ideas. For example, if your own family is not religious, you could give examples of how important your family is to you and your parents.

Topic 3.7.3 Hinduism and family life

Family life is important in Hinduism because:

- According to the teachings on ashrama, every Hindu must go through the householder stage of life. Unless a Hindu performs his/her duties as a householder and raises a family, they will not achieve moksha. So Hinduism sees the family as a duty everyone must take part in to reach nirvana.
- Hinduism also teaches that the family was created as the basic unit of society and as the only place in which children should be brought up. Therefore it is the most important part of society and without the family society would collapse.
- Hinduism teaches that the family is the place where children learn the difference between right and wrong, so without the family there would be much more evil in the world.
- In Hinduism, the family is the place where children are introduced to the faith through daily puja, being taken to mandir, celebrating festivals, and so on. This means that the family is very important for Hinduism to continue and grow.
- The Hindu scriptures outline the nature of Hindu family life and show its importance. Hindus should follow the guidance of the scriptures and so should see the importance of family life.

> *Where the women are respected, there lives God. If the wife is obedient to the husband and the husband loves his wife; if the children obey the parents, and guests are entertained; if the family duty is performed and gifts are given to the needy, then there is heaven and nowhere else.*
>
> **The Laws of Manu**

Worshipping (puja) at the family **shrine** brings the family together.

Questions

b Do you think family life is important? Give two reasons for your point of view. **4**

c Choose one religion other than Christianity and explain why family life is important in that religion. **8**

d 'Family life is more important for religious people than for non-religious people.'

   i Do you agree? Give reasons for your opinion. **3**

   ii Give reasons why some people may disagree with you. **3**

Exam Tip

d Remember to use the techniques for answering evaluation questions on page 9. Arguments for the statement would be the reasons in this topic. Arguments against would have to come from your class discussion or your own ideas. For example, if your own family is not religious, you could give examples of how important your family is to you and your parents.

SUMMARY

Family life is important in Hinduism because Hinduism teaches that the family is the basis of society and raising a family is part of the dharma of the householder stage of life.

Topic 3.7.4 Sikhism and family life

> Family life is superior to the ascetic life (being a monk/holy man).
>
> **Guru Granth Sahib 586**

> It is the greatest sin to quarrel with parents who have given you birth and brought you up.
>
> **Guru Granth Sahib 1200**

A Sikh family.

SUMMARY

The family is important in Sikhism because it was created by God to keep society together, and the family is the main way of keeping Sikhism alive.

Family life is important in Sikhism because:
- Sikhism teaches that the family was created by God as the basic unit of society and as the only place in which children should be brought up. Therefore it is the most important part of society and without the family society would collapse.
- Sikhs believe that God is present in the home and the Guru Granth Sahib often refers to God as 'our father and mother' showing how important the family should be for Sikhs.
- The human Gurus married and had families, showing how important the family is. Sikhs should follow the example of the human Gurus and so it is tremendously important for Sikhs to take part in family life.
- The Guru Granth Sahib teaches that family life is the highest form of life. As the Guru Granth Sahib is the living Guru for Sikhs, they must also see family life as the highest form of life.
- Sikhism teaches that the family is the place where children learn the difference between right and wrong, so without the family there would be much more evil in the world.
- In Sikhism, the family is the place where children are introduced to the faith through the naming ceremony, praying at home, being taken to the **gurdwara**, celebrating festivals, and so on. This means that the family is very important for Sikhism to continue and grow.

Questions
b Do you think family life is important? Give two reasons for your point of view. **4**
c Choose one religion other than Christianity and explain why family life is important in that religion. **8**
d 'Family life is more important for religious people than for non-religious people.'
   i Do you agree? Give reasons for your opinion. **3**
   ii Give reasons why some people may disagree with you. **3**

Exam Tip
d Remember to use the techniques for answering evaluation questions on page 9. Arguments for the statement would be the reasons in this topic. Arguments against would have to come from your class discussion or your own ideas. For example, if your own family is not religious, you could give examples of how important your family is to you and your parents.

Topic 3.8 Christian attitudes to homosexuality

There are several attitudes to homosexuality in Christianity. The main ones are:

1. The Catholic attitude

The Catholic attitude towards homosexuality is that being a homosexual is not a sin but that homosexual sexual relationships are a sin. The Catholic Church asks homosexuals to live without any sexual activity (i.e. be celibate). They believe that the sacraments of the Church will help them do this. The Catholic Church condemns all forms of homophobia. It believes it is sinful to criticise homosexuals or attack their behaviour.

Catholics have this attitude because:
- The Bible condemns homosexual sexual activity.
- It is the tradition of the Church that sexual activity should be creative as well as unitive, and it is not possible for homosexuals to have creative sex.
- It is the teaching of the Magisterium found in the Catechism of the Catholic Church, which Catholics should believe.
- The Church teaches that people cannot help their sexual orientation (but they can control their sexual activity). Therefore discriminating against people because of their sexual orientation is similar to racism, which the Church regards as sinful.

Christians, Jews and Muslims joined forces to campaign against the Gay Rights Bill in January 2007. Here a group of Christian protestors sing hymns.

It is necessary to distinguish between sexual orientation or inclination and indulging in sexual (genital) activity, homosexual or heterosexual. Neither a homosexual nor a heterosexual orientation leads inevitably to sexual activity. Furthermore, an individual's sexual orientation can be unclear, even complex. Also, it may vary over the years. Being a homosexual person is, then, neither morally good nor morally bad: it is homosexual genital acts that are morally wrong ... The Church does not consider the whole personality and character of the individual to be thereby disordered. Homosexual people, as well as heterosexual people, can, and often do, give a fine example of friendship and the art of chaste loving.

A note on the teaching of the Catholic Church concerning homosexual people, Cardinal Hume 1995

The Church utterly condemns all forms of unjust discrimination, violence, harassment or abuse directed against people who are homosexual. Consequently, the Church teaches that homosexual people 'must be accepted with respect, compassion, and sensitivity'.

Cherishing Life, Catholic Bishops' Conference of England and Wales 2004

A civil partnership requires:

- both partners to provide reasonable maintenance for their civil partner and any children of the family
- civil partners to be assessed in the same way as husbands and wives for child support
- equal treatment for the purposes of life assurance, employment and pension benefits and recognition for immigration and nationality purposes.

The issue of homosexuality has caused major divisions in the Anglican Church (Churches in communion with the Church of England) since the Episcopal Church of the USA appointed an openly gay priest, Gene Robinson, as Bishop of New Hampshire. The Lambeth Conference declared in 1998 that homosexuals in a relationship should not be ordained as priests, and in 2004 called on the US Episcopal Church to repent for consecrating an openly gay bishop.

Compiled from news stories

If all the gay people stayed away from church on a given Sunday, the Church of England would be close to shut down, between its organists, its clergy, its wardens ... it seems less than humble not to admit that.

Right Rev Gene Robinson interviewed in London, July 2007

2. The Evangelical Protestant attitude

Many Evangelical Protestants believe that homosexuality is a sin. They believe that there should be no homosexual Christians and hold special prayer meetings to give homosexuals the power of the Holy spirit to change their sexual preference (orientation). The reasons for this attitude are:

- They believe that the Bible is the direct word of God and as the Bible condemns homosexuality in some passages of both the Old and New Testaments, it must be wrong.
- They believe that the **salvation** of Christ can remove all sins, including homosexuality.
- They believe it because all the Churches have taught it, even though some now say homosexuality is acceptable.

However, the Evangelical Alliance has recently made this statement: 'At the same time we utterly repudiate homophobia and call upon churches to welcome those of a homosexual orientation as they would welcome any other person.'

The Right Reverend Gene Robinson, who is the ninth bishop of New Hampshire in the Episcopal Church in the United States of America. He became the first openly gay bishop inside the wider Anglican Church in 2003. Should an openly gay man be appointed bishop?

3. The Liberal Protestant attitude

Many Liberal Protestants have the attitude that lifelong homosexual relationships are acceptable and homosexuals are therefore welcomed into the Church, but homosexual relationships cannot be equal to Christian marriage. It is accepted that Ministers/priests may have a homosexual orientation but they must not take part in homosexual sex. Some Liberal Protestants provide blessings for civil partnerships.

The reasons for this attitude are:

- They believe that the teachings of the Bible need re-interpreting in the light of modern knowledge and that the anti-homosexual texts in the Bible are a reflection of the Jewish culture at the time rather than the word of God.
- They feel that the major Christian belief in love and acceptance means that homosexuals must be accepted.
- Many believe that inspiration comes from the Holy Spirit as well as the Bible and if Christians feel the Spirit approves of their homosexuality, it cannot be denied.
- They believe that Christians should be open and honest and refusing rights to gay Christians encourages them to be dishonest and hypocritical about their nature and life.

Some Christian ministers and priests will give a church blessing for a civil partnership. Is this a good idea?

Questions

b Do you think homosexuals should have equal rights? Give two reasons for your point of view. **4**

c Explain why some Christians accept homosexuality and some do not. **8**

d 'No Christian should be homosexual.'
  - i Do you agree? Give reasons for your opinion. **3**
  - ii Give reasons why some people may disagree with you. **3**

Exam Tip

d Remember to use the techniques for answering evaluation questions on page 9. Arguments for the statement would be the reasons for the Evangelical Protestant view. Arguments against would be the reasons for the Liberal Protestant view.

SUMMARY

- Catholics believe there is nothing wrong with homosexual feelings or relationships as long as there is no sexual activity because this is the teaching of the Church.
- Evangelical Protestants believe that homosexuality is sinful because it is condemned in the Bible.
- Liberal Protestants believe that homosexuality is acceptable because it is natural and Christians should love and accept everyone.

Topic 3.9.1 Muslim attitudes to homosexuality

As Dr Zaki Badawi of the Muslim College, London, points out, the fact that homosexuality is incompatible with Islam does not mean gays or lesbians can be denied the right to call themselves Muslims, 'We can say that homosexuals are not good Muslims because they are practising an unacceptable sin but we cannot completely write them out of Islam. As long as they believe in Allah and the Messenger (peace be upon Him) none other than Allah has the authority to deny them their Islamic identity.'

1. The majority attitude

Most Muslims believe homosexuality is wrong because:
- Homosexuality is condemned by the Qur'an and the Qur'an is the final word of God, which all Muslims should obey.
- The Prophet Muhammad condemned homosexuality in several hadith. As Muhammad was the last prophet and the perfect example for Muslims, Muslims should follow his teachings.
- God declared in the Qur'an that marriage between a man and a woman is the only lawful form of sex, therefore homosexual sex must be wrong.
- Islam teaches that the primary aim of sex is to have children and as homosexual sex has no possibility of creating children, it must be wrong.
- The family is the heart of Islam, but homosexuality denies the possibility of family life and so it must be wrong.

2. The minority attitude

Some Muslims believe that homosexuality is acceptable because:
- They believe that Islam is a religion of tolerance, not hate, and therefore Muslims should be tolerant of those of a different sexual orientation.
- They believe that God created all people and loves them as he created them.
- They believe that scientific evidence about homosexuality means that people are born homosexual, therefore God must have made them homosexual and must want them to be homosexual.

Questions
b Do you think religions should accept homosexuality? Give two reasons for your point of view. **4**
c Choose one religion other than Christianity and explain why some of its followers are against homosexuality, but others are not. **8**
d 'No religious person should ever be homosexual.'
   i Do you agree? Give reasons for your opinion. **3**
   ii Give reasons why some people may disagree with you. **3**

Exam Tip
c 'Explain' means give reasons. To answer this question you should use two of the above reasons for Muslims being against homosexuality, and two of the above reasons for some Muslims not being against homosexuality, and make each of them into a short paragraph. For tips on Quality of Written Communication, look at page 3.

SUMMARY
- Most Muslims believe homosexuality is wrong because it is condemned in the Qur'an and Shari'ah.
- A few Muslims believe that homosexuality should be accepted because it was created by God and Islam is a religion of peace and tolerance.

Topic 3.9.2 Jewish attitudes to homosexuality

There are two different attitudes to homosexuality in Judaism.

1. The Orthodox Jewish view is that homosexual activity is wrong, but homosexual orientation is not wrong and homophobia is condemned very strongly. They are against homosexual activity because:
   - The Torah condemns homosexual activity and the Torah is the word of God, whose commands must be obeyed by Orthodox Jews.
   - The Torah and Talmud declare that marriage between a man and a woman is the only lawful form of sex, therefore homosexual sex must be wrong.
   - Judaism teaches that the primary aim of sex is to have children and as homosexual sex has no possibility of creating children, it must be wrong.
   - It is a mitzvot that Jewish adults should marry and raise a family to continue the Jewish race and faith. All Orthodox Jews must fulfil the mitzvot and as homosexuals cannot, it follows that homosexuality must be wrong.

2. The Liberal or reform groups see homosexuality as acceptable and there have been homosexual rabbis. Nevertheless they still see heterosexual marriage as the ideal state. They have this attitude because:
   - They believe that the Torah needs to be re-interpreted in the light of the modern world.
   - As scientists now believe that sexual orientation is genetic it must be natural and so God-given.
   - The Rabbis teach that Jewish people should treat others as they would want to be treated themselves, which must mean accepting homosexuals.
   - They feel that labelling homosexuality as wrong leads to homophobia, which is closely linked to the evils of racism.

Rabbi Lionel Blue was the first openly gay Jewish rabbi in the UK.

As Liberal Jews we believe that a loving, monogamous relationship deserves to be sanctified in front of one's family and community. Liberal Judaism encourages couples who choose to have a civil partnership to affirm their relationship with a religious ceremony. The ceremony might look very traditional, with the couple celebrating their commitment to one another under a chuppah (the Jewish marriage canopy), or it might be a specially designed ceremony.

Statement submitted to the *Report on Faiths and Homophobia*, London 2007

Questions

b Do you think religions should accept homosexuality? Give two reasons for your point of view. **4**

c Choose one religion other than Christianity and explain why some of its followers are against homosexuality, but others are not. **8**

d 'No religious person should ever be homosexual.'
   i Do you agree? Give reasons for your opinion. **3**
   ii Give reasons why some people may disagree with you. **3**

Exam Tip

c 'Explain' means give reasons. To answer this question you should use two of the above reasons for Jewish people being against homosexuality, and two of the above reasons for some Jewish people not being against homosexuality, and make each of them into a short paragraph. For tips on Quality of Written Communication, look at page 3.

SUMMARY

- Orthodox Jews believe homosexuality is wrong because it is condemned in the Torah and stops people from having children.
- Most Liberal/Reform Jews accept homosexuality because it is natural and Jewish people should respect others.

Topic 3.9.3 Hindu attitudes to homosexuality

A Hijra march in Bombay 2004 to protest against unfair treatment by the Indian authorities.

I am the power of those who are strong, when this power is free from passions and selfish desires. I am desire when this is pure, when this desire is not against righteousness.

Bhagavad Gita 7:11

When the tip of a hair is split into a hundred parts, and one of those parts further into a hundred parts – the individual soul, on the one hand, is the size of one such part, and, on the other, it partakes of infinity. It is neither a woman nor a man, nor even a hermaphrodite; it is ruled over by whatever body it obtains.

Svetasavatara Upanishad 5:9–10

SUMMARY

- Most Hindus believe that homosexuality is wrong because it stops people from fulfilling their duty as householders.
- Some Hindus accept homosexuality because it is natural and could be another way of finding moksha.

There are two attitudes to homosexuality in Hinduism.

1 Most Hindus disapprove of homosexuality and think it should not be practised by Hindus. They have this attitude because:
   - The Laws of Manu only mention and approve of heterosexual sex, therefore homosexuality must be wrong.
   - All Hindus should pass through the second ashrama, which is the householder stage. To be a householder one must marry and raise a family, neither of which a homosexual can do.
   - Hinduism restricts sexual activity to the householder stage and as homosexuals cannot be a householder, they should not have sex.
   - As homosexuals cannot perform their dharma as householders, they will not be able to attain moksha.

2 Some Hindus believe that homosexuals should be treated the same as heterosexuals. They have this attitude because:
   - There are sculptures and carvings of homosexual sex (both male and female) in old Hindu temples showing that homosexuality was thought of as holy and as a way of communicating with God.
   - There are ways other than the fulfilment of dharma by which to achieve moksha, and homosexuals find it easier to spend time concentrating on God.
   - There is a special **caste** called the Hijras. They are men who dress and behave as women (often castrating themselves) to serve the mother goddess Parvati. They show that sexuality is not easily defined.
   - As scientists now believe that sexual orientation is genetic it must be natural and so God-given.

Questions
b Do you think religions should accept homosexuality? Give two reasons for your point of view. **4**
c Choose one religion other than Christianity and explain why some of its followers are against homosexuality, but others are not. **8**
d 'No religious person should ever be homosexual.'
   i Do you agree? Give reasons for your opinion. **3**
   ii Give reasons why some people may disagree with you. **3**

Exam Tip
c 'Explain' means give reasons. To answer this question you should use two of the above reasons for Hindus being against homosexuality, and two of the above reasons for some Hindus not being against homosexuality, and make each of them into a short paragraph. For tips on Quality of Written Communication, look at page 3.

Topic 3.9.4 Sikh attitudes to homosexuality

There are two different attitudes to homosexuality in Sikhism, neither of which could claim to be the official view as neither the Guru Granth Sahib, nor the Rahit Maryada say anything about homosexuality.

1 Many Sikhs still think that homosexuality is wrong and that it is possible to change sexual orientation by prayer and self-control. They have this attitude because:

- Sikhism expects all Sikhs to marry and raise a family. Homosexuals cannot do this and so homosexuality must be wrong.
- The human Gurus married and had families, showing they were heterosexual. Sikhs should follow the example of the human Gurus and so they too should marry and have families, which can only be done by heterosexuals.
- Although the Gurus and the Rahit Maryada do not mention homosexuality, they do restrict sex to marriage. As homosexuals cannot marry, it follows that the teachings of the Sikh authorities say that homosexuals should not have sex.

2 Some Sikhs accept homosexuality and think homosexuals should be treated the same as anyone else. They have this attitude because:

- If homosexuality is wrong it would have been banned by the Guru Granth Sahib or the Rahit Maryada.
- They believe that homosexuality should be governed by the same Sikh rules as heterosexuality. Therefore Sikh homosexuals should be faithful to one partner.
- As scientists now believe that sexual orientation is genetic it must be natural and so God-given. Sikhs should respect all of God's creation and so homosexuals should be respected.

Basically, the relationship between men and women is very sacred and the ideal of joining two souls to realise God together. Homosexuality is not talked about in the scriptures and also in the lives of ten Gurus over a period of 200 years.

Jasvinder Singh, ex-president of a gurdwara, answering the question, 'What stance does Sikhism take on the issue of homosexuality?'

I am a gay man and was seeing another man who is a Sikh for a number of years. After much pressure, he ended our relationship as apparently it was against his religion. It is my belief that Sikhism needs to adapt to the twenty-first century and put up with everyone. How can they expect to be accepted if they are not willing to accept others? By way of a footnote, my ex is now married and by all accounts very unhappy.

Martin, London
Letter responding to a BBC debate on Sikhism

Questions

b Do you think religions should accept homosexuality? Give two reasons for your point of view. **4**

c Choose one religion other than Christianity and explain why some of its followers are against homosexuality, but others are not. **8**

d 'No religious person should ever be homosexual.'
  i Do you agree? Give reasons for your opinion. **3**
  ii Give reasons why some people may disagree with you. **3**

Exam Tip

c 'Explain' means give reasons. To answer this question you should use two of the above reasons for Sikhs being against homosexuality, and two of the above reasons for some Sikhs not being against homosexuality, and make each of them into a short paragraph. For tips on Quality of Written Communication, look at page 3.

SUMMARY

- Most Sikhs believe that homosexuality is wrong because it stops people from marrying and raising a family.
- Some Sikhs accept homosexuality because it is natural and is not mentioned in the Sikh scriptures.

Topic 3.10 Different Christian attitudes to contraception

In July 1987, at a conference on responsible procreation, Pope John Paul II reminded Christians attending that *Humanae Vitae* affirms the Church's consistent and historical teaching that there is an 'inseparable connection, willed by God and unable to be broken by man on his own initiative, between the two meanings of the conjugal act (married sexual act); the unitive and the procreative.'

The methods of birth regulation based on self-observation and the use of infertile periods ... respect the bodies of the spouses, encourage tenderness between them ... In contrast, 'every action which, whether in anticipation of the conjugal act, or in its accomplishment, or in the development of its natural consequences, proposes, whether as an end or as a means, to render procreation impossible' is intrinsically evil.

Catechism of the Catholic Church 2370

Throughout history people have tried to control the number of children that they have for a number of reasons:
- for the health of the mother
- to provide more food for the family unit
- to provide a better standard of living for the family unit.

Condoms were developed in the nineteenth century but the contraceptive pill was developed in the 1950s and gradually became the main form of artificial **contraception** used. Since the rise of cases of AIDS/HIV, condoms have been recommended as a safe method of having sex.

There are two main attitudes to contraception among Christians.

1. The Catholic attitude

The Catholic Church has always taught responsible parenthood. The Church teaches that sexual intercourse is a gift from God as a source of joy and pleasure to married couples (the unitive purpose) as well as a means of creating a family (the creative purpose). Responsible parenthood involves deciding on the number of children to have and when to have them. However, the Catholic way to achieve this is through using natural family planning (restricting sex to the infertile period of a woman's menstrual cycle). The Church teaches that using artificial methods of contraception is going against God's intentions. Catholics believe this because:

- In *Casti Connubii*, published in 1930, Pope Pius XI condemned all forms of artificial contraception.
- In 1951 Pope Pius XII declared that Catholics could use natural methods of contraception as these are natural and so part of God's creation.
- In 1968, Pope Paul VI's encyclical *Humanae Vitae* affirmed the teaching of previous Popes that the only allowable forms of contraception are natural methods. This teaching has been confirmed in the Catechism of the Catholic Church.

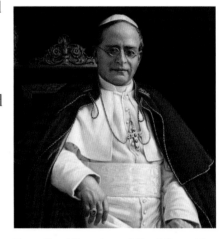

Pope Pius XI, author of *Casti Connubii*

- Artificial methods of birth control separate the unitive and creative aspects of sex, which is not what God intended.
- Some contraceptives have abortifacient effects (they bring about a very early abortion) and so are against the teaching of the Church.
- The Catholic Church regards contraception as a major cause of sexual promiscuity, broken families, the rise in the divorce rate and sexually transmitted diseases.

2. The attitude of non-Catholic Christians

Almost all non-Catholic Christians believe that all forms of contraception are permissible as long as they are used to restrict the size of the family and not simply to stop having children altogether. They have this attitude because:

- Christianity is about love and justice, and contraception improves women's health and raises the standard of living of children as families are smaller.
- God created sex for enjoyment and to cement the bonds of marriage. Within marriage, contraception allows the role of sex to be separated from making children and this is not against God's will.
- There is nothing in the Bible that forbids the use of contraception.
- In 1930, the Lambeth Conference of the worldwide Anglican Communion (**Church of England**) declared it was legitimate for Christians to use contraception to limit family size. This has been followed by the major Protestant Churches and the Orthodox Churches.
- They believe that it is better to combat AIDS/HIV by using condoms than by expecting everyone to follow Christian rules about sex and marriage.

Contraception is seen as a gift from medical science under God's sovereignty. Choosing not to have or space families is morally defensible, considering the needs of the world, population size and family responsibility. However, those contraceptives that have an abortifacient function (for example, IUD and various pills) are considered to take human life and should be avoided.

Statement by the Baptist Church in *What the Churches Say*

Questions

b Do you think contraception should be used? Give two reasons for your point of view. **4**

c Explain why some Christians allow artificial methods of contraception and some do not. **8**

d 'Christians should never use contraceptives.'
  i Do you agree? Give reasons for your opinion. **3**
  ii Give reasons why some people may disagree with you. **3**

Exam Tip

b You should already have thought about this, and you just have to give two reasons for your opinion. For example, if you agree with contraception, you could use two reasons for non-Catholic Churches agreeing with contraception.

SUMMARY

The Catholic Church teaches that using artificial methods of contraception to stop a baby being conceived is wrong. God gave sex in order to create children. Other Christians allow the use of contraception because they believe God gave sex to strengthen a married relationship.

Topic 3.11.1 Muslim attitudes to contraception

A Muslim family.

If Allah wishes to create a child, you cannot prevent it.

Hadith reported by four authorities

Contraception is not like abortion. Abortion is a crime against an existing being.

Imam Al-Ghazzali

SUMMARY

- Some Muslims are against the use of contraceptives because they believe God created sex for procreation.
- Other Muslims agree with contraception because the Prophet and law schools do.

All Muslims believe that contraception should not be used to prevent Muslims having any children, but there are different attitudes as to whether contraception can be used to limit family size.

1 Some Muslims believe that contraception is going against the will of God and should not be used at all by Muslims. They have this attitude because:
- Although the Qur'an does not refer to contraception explicitly, Muslims opposed to birth control believe that the verse, 'You should not kill your children for fear of want' means a ban on contraception as well as infanticide.
- They believe that God created sex for procreation and therefore contraception is against God's wishes.
- They are opposed to abortion and so would not allow any contraceptives that acted as abortifacients.
- They believe it is the duty of Muslims to have large families.

2 Some Muslims believe that it is permitted for Muslims to use contraception to limit family size and to prevent harm to the health of the mother. They have this attitude because:
- There are several hadith which record that the Prophet permitted the use of **coitus interruptus** as a means of contraception. From this the majority of the law schools have argued that artificial methods of contraception are permitted for Muslims.
- There are several verses in the Qur'an where God says he does not place extra burdens on his followers, and a large family places extra burdens on the mother and father, therefore contraception must be allowed.
- If pregnancy is likely to result in the mother's death, contraception must be allowed because not to use it would be like suicide, which is banned in the Qur'an.
- Muslim lawyers agree that contraception is different from abortion and so should be permitted.

Questions

b Do you think religions should allow their followers to use contraceptives? Give two reasons for your point of view. **4**

c Choose one religion other than Christianity and explain why some of its followers accept any form of contraception and some do not. **8**

d 'No religious person should use artificial methods of contraception.'
   i Do you agree? Give reasons for your opinion. **3**
   ii Give reasons why some people may disagree with you. **3**

Exam Tip

d Remember to use the techniques for answering evaluation questions on page 9. Arguments for the statement would be the reasons for the traditional Muslim view. Arguments against would be the reasons for the Liberal Muslim view.

Topic 3.11.2 Jewish attitudes to contraception

There are three different attitudes to contraception in Judaism:

1 The Ultra Orthodox: Very Orthodox Jews do not approve of any form of artificial contraception, however, if the mother's health is at risk, these Jews would discuss contraception with their Rabbi and doctor. They have this attitude because:

- God commanded the Jewish people to be fruitful and populate the earth, therefore they should have large families.
- The Torah makes it clear that God regards the male sperm as sacred and not to be killed.
- Many Rabbis have taught that God created sex primarily for procreation.

2 The Orthodox: Orthodox Jews allow women to use artificial methods of contraception after a couple has had at least two children because:

- Torah, Talmud and the rabbis teach that the health of the mother should come first and so contraceptives can be used to preserve the health of the mother.
- Contraceptives for women do not kill the male seed and so do not go against the Torah.
- It is a mitzvot to marry and have children to carry on the Jewish faith, but this does not require more than two children.
- Use of condoms to protect against HIV and sexually transmitted diseases would have to be discussed with the Rabbi before use.

3 The Liberal/Reform: Liberal/Reform Jews believe that individuals have the right to make their own moral decisions about contraception:

- God expects people to use intelligence and technology to prevent unwanted things from happening. If a couple does not want to have children, they can use contraception.
- They believe the Torah's teaching on male sperm needs to be updated. Men and women are equal and contraception should be available to either.
- Ideally all Jewish people should marry and have children, but it is better to use contraception than bring unwanted children into the world.

> *Then God blessed Noah and his sons, saying to them, 'Be fruitful and increase in number and fill the earth.'*
>
> **Genesis 9:1**

SUMMARY

- Ultra Orthodox Jews do not allow contraception because they believe God wants them to have large families.
- Orthodox Jews allow only female contraception because the Torah says the male seed is sacred.
- Liberal/Reform Jews allow any form of contraception because they believe the Torah should be brought up to date.

Exam Tip

c Remember to use the techniques for answering evaluation questions on page 9. Arguments for the statement would be the reasons for the Orthodox view. Arguments against would be the reasons for the Liberal/Reform view.

Questions

b Do you think religions should allow their followers to use contraceptives? Give two reasons for your point of view. **4**

c Choose one religion other than Christianity and explain why some of its followers accept any form of contraception and some do not. **8**

d 'No religious person should use artificial methods of contraception.'
  i Do you agree? Give reasons for your opinion. **3**
  ii Give reasons why some people may disagree with you. **3**

Topic 3.11.3 Hindu attitudes to contraception

When a man deposits the semen in a woman ... it becomes one with the woman's body as if it were part of her own body.

Aitareya Upanishad 2:2

Why would many Hindus take notice of this poster?

SUMMARY

- Most Hindus believe in contraception because it does not affect the soul and it helps the population not to exceed the food supply.
- Some Hindus only accept contraceptives which do not kill sperm or eggs because of their beliefs in ahimsa.
- A few Hindus are against all forms of contraception because they believe it is the duty of a householder to have a large family.

Exam Tip

d Remember to use the techniques for answering evaluation questions on page 9. Arguments for the statement would be the reasons for the traditional Hindu view. Arguments against would be the reasons for the Liberal Hindu view.

There are three attitudes to contraception in Hinduism:

1 Most Hindus believe that all forms of contraception are good and should be used to limit family size. Many Hindus in India are sterilised after two children to try to reduce the population explosion. They have this attitude because:
- They believe that children should be a joy and not a burden. The householder ashrama should be about fulfilling one's dharma, not struggling to cope with a large family.
- They believe the soul does not enter the body until after conception and so the soul cannot be affected by contraception.
- They believe that humans should use their intelligence and technology to improve life and to make sure that the population does not exceed the food supply.
- They believe that contraception is different from abortion, it does not involve violence to a living thing and so it is not against ahimsa.

2 Some Hindus only accept certain forms of contraception, such as the pill and sterilisation. They have this attitude because:
- They believe strongly in ahimsa and think that any form of contraception that involves killing either sperm or eggs is an unacceptable form of violence.
- They are against abortion and so cannot accept abortifacient forms of contraception.

3 A few Hindus are against any form of contraception. They have this attitude because:
- They believe that large families should be part of the householder ashrama.
- They believe that sex must involve the possibility of procreation to fulfil one's dharma. They believe strongly in ahimsa and think that any form of contraception that involves killing either sperm or eggs is an unacceptable form of violence.
- They are against abortion and so cannot accept abortifacient forms of contraception.

Questions

b Do you think religions should allow their followers to use contraceptives? Give two reasons for your point of view. **4**
c Choose one religion other than Christianity and explain why some of its followers accept any form of contraception and some do not. **8**
d 'No religious person should use artificial methods of contraception.'
   i Do you agree? Give reasons for your opinion. **3**
   ii Give reasons why some people may disagree with you. **3**

Topic 3.11.4 Sikh attitudes to contraception

There are different attitudes to contraception among Sikhs.

1 Some Sikhs think that it is wrong to use contraceptives whatever the reasons for doing so. They have this view because:
   • They believe that God gave sex to humans to have children and so every act of sex should be open to new life.
   • They believe contraception is killing life and the Guru Granth Sahib says that Sikhs should not take life.
   • They believe that Sikhs should follow the example of the human Gurus who had large families.

A child is born when it pleases God.
Guru Granth Sahib 921

2 Most Sikhs believe contraceptives can be used by married couples to limit family size, but only after they have had two children. They have this view because:
   • They do not think that contraception takes life because they believe life does not begin until the moment of conception.
   • They think it is not necessary to have large families or risk the wife's health because the Guru Granth Sahib says that God does not intend humans to suffer.
   • They believe that Sikhs should have a family because the Gurus had families and Sikhs should follow the examples of the Gurus.

3 Some Sikhs think that contraception can be used by a married couple without any restrictions. They have this attitude because:
   • Contraception is not mentioned in the Guru Granth Sahib or the Rahit Maryada and what is not banned by these must be permitted.
   • They believe that the teaching of the Guru Granth Sahib on God not wanting humans to suffer unnecessarily means that they should not have to have children until they are ready.

Questions

b Do you think religions should allow their followers to use contraceptives? Give two reasons for your point of view. **4**

c Choose one religion other than Christianity and explain why some of its followers accept any form of contraception and some do not. **8**

d 'No religious person should use artificial methods of contraception.'
   i Do you agree? Give reasons for your opinion. **3**
   ii Give reasons why some people may disagree with you. **3**

Exam Tip

d Remember to use the techniques for answering evaluation questions on page 9. Arguments for the statement would be the reasons for the traditional Sikh view. Arguments against would be the reasons for the Liberal Sikh view.

SUMMARY

• Some Sikhs beleive contraception is wrong because all sex should allow for the procreation of life.

• Most Sikhs believe contraception can be used to limit family size after two children.

• Some Sikhs believe a married couple can use contraception because it is not mentioned in the Sikh holy book.

How to answer exam questions

Question A **What is a re-constituted family?**　　2 marks

Where two sets of children (step-brothers and sisters) become one family when their divorced parents marry each other.

Question B **Do you think contraception should be used?**
Give two reasons for your point of view.　　4 marks

Yes I do because there is nothing in the Bible that forbids the use of contraception so Christians can use it. Also contraception makes families happier. The mother has time for the children because she is not pregnant all the time, and the family will have more money.

Question C **Choose one religion other than Christianity and explain why family life is important in that religion.**　　8 marks

Family life is important in Islam because Islam teaches that the family was created by God to keep society together. If the family was created by God, it must be important.

Muslims believe that the family is the only way approved by God to bring up children. Therefore the family must be important because society needs children.

Muslims also believe the family is important because it is in the family that children learn about Islam and are taught how to follow the Five Pillars, by praying at home, giving zakah, fasting in Ramadan and learning about hajj.

Perhaps the main reason why the family is important in Islam is because all Muslims try to follow the example of the Prophet Muhammad. Muhammad was married and had a family and so it is very important for Muslims also to marry and have a family.

Question D **'A religious wedding ceremony helps to make a marriage work.'**

　i Do you agree? Give reasons for your opinion.　　3 marks

　ii Give reasons why some people may disagree with you.　　3 marks

i I do not agree because I believe that love is what makes a marriage work. It seems to me that just as many people who have a religious wedding ceremony get divorced as those who do not have a religious wedding ceremony. If you make a promise to stay with someone you love, you will not break that promise whether you make it to God as well or not. People who have affairs do not seem to think, 'God will punish me for this'. So I disagree with the statement.

ii Many Christians would disagree with me. They believe that a religious wedding ceremony helps to make a marriage work because the couple make promises to God to stay together and breaking that promise would be like lying to God. Also at the ceremony prayers are said by a priest asking God's blessing and so God will be helping to make the marriage work. Finally they get advice at the ceremony from the Bible and the priest about how to make the marriage work.

Introduction

This section of the examination specification requires you to look at issues surrounding the roles of men and women, racial harmony, religious harmony and the media and community cohesion.

Roles of men and women

You will need to understand the effects of, and give reasons for your own opinion about:

- how and why attitudes to the roles of men and women have changed in the United Kingdom
- different Christian attitudes to equal rights for women in religion
- different attitudes to equal rights for women in religion in one religion other than Christianity.

Racial harmony

You will need to understand the effects of, and give reasons for your own opinion about:

- the nature of the United Kingdom as a multi-ethnic society
- government action to promote community cohesion in the United Kingdom
- why Christians should help to promote racial harmony
- why the followers of one religion other than Christianity should help to promote racial harmony.

Religious harmony

You will need to understand the effects of, and give reasons for your own opinion about:

- the United Kingdom as a multi-faith society
- issues raised for religion by a multi-faith society
- ways in which religions work to promote community cohesion in the United Kingdom.

The media and community cohesion

You will need to understand the effects of, and give reasons for your own opinion about how an issue from religion and community cohesion has been presented in one form of the media and whether the treatment was fair to religious beliefs and religious people.

101

Topic 4.1 How and why attitudes to the roles of men and women have changed in the United Kingdom

Women make up 84 per cent of employees in personal services (care assistants, child minders, hairdressers, etc).

Men make up 66 per cent of managers, senior officials, professionals.

Source: Census 2001

Statistics

The gender pay gap (the difference between men's and women's median hourly pay) is narrowing:

1986	26%
2002	19%
2007	12.6%

Average minutes spent per day

Activity	Men	Women
Cooking	27	54
Cleaning	13	47
Laundry	4	18
Caring for children	22	42

Source: National Statistics

How attitudes have changed

Women in the UK have always had the right to own property and earn their own living, but they did not have the same rights as men and when women married, their husbands had the right to use their property. During the second half of the nineteenth century, it became the accepted view that married women should stay at home and look after the children (in 1850 about 50 per cent of married women had been in employment, but by 1900 this was down to about 15 per cent).

However, women began to fight to have equal rights with men. The growth of equal rights for women began with the Married Women's Property Act 1882, which allowed married women to keep their property separate from their husband's. In 1892, the Local Government Act gave women the right to stand as councillors. However, it was not until 1928 that the Electoral Reform Act gave equal voting rights to women, and allowed women to stand as MPs.

Equal rights in employment did not arrive until the Equal Pay Act of 1970, which required employers to give women the same pay as men – equal pay for like work regardless of the employee's sex. Then, in 1975, the Sex Discrimination Act made it illegal to discriminate in employment on grounds of gender or whether someone is married (though religion was given an opt-out). These Acts gave women the right to take employers to court if they treated them differently.

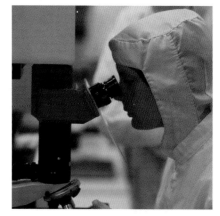

A female technician. How does this image show changing attitudes to the role of women?

Although women achieved equal rights in law, attitudes to the roles of men and women have been even slower to change.

Men's attitudes to the roles of men and women have changed considerably – in 1989, 32 per cent of men agreed that, 'a man's job is to earn money, a woman's job is to look after the home and family' whereas in

2008 only 17 per cent of men agreed with the statement. However, there has been less progress in who actually does the work around the home. Sixty-eight per cent of women say they do all the housework, though only 54 per cent of men agree.

Why attitudes have changed

- During the First and Second World Wars, women had to take on many of the jobs previously done by men and proved they could do them just as well.
- The development of equal rights for women in other countries (New Zealand was the first country to give women equal political rights) made it difficult to claim it was not needed.
- The success of women as councillors and the important contribution of women to developments in health and social care showed that women were the equals of men in these areas.
- The work of the suffragette movement to gain equal voting and political rights for women showed the men in authority that women were no longer prepared to be treated as second class citizens.
- Social and industrial developments in the 1950s and 1960s led the need for more women workers and for married women to provide a second income.
- The UN Declaration of Human Rights and the development of the Feminist Movement put forward a case for equal rights that could not be contradicted.
- The Labour governments of 1964–70 and 1974–79 were dedicated to the equal rights campaign and passed the Equal Pay Act and the Sex Discrimination Act.

Why might this have surprised people in 1943?

> *Everyone is entitled to all the rights and freedoms set forth in this Declaration, without distinction of any kind, such as race, colour, sex, language, religion, political or other opinion, national or social origin, property, birth or other status. Furthermore, no distinction shall be made on the basis of the political, jurisdictional or international status of the country or territory to which a person belongs, whether it be independent, trust, non-self-governing or under any other limitation of sovereignty.*

Article 2 of the UN Declaration of Human Rights

Questions

b Do you think men should share housework with women? Give two reasons for your point of view. **4**

c Explain how attitudes to the roles of men and women have changed. **8**

d 'Men and women should have equal roles in life.'
  i Do you agree? Give reasons for your opinion. **3**
  ii Give reasons why some people may disagree with you. **3**

Exam Tip

c 'Explain' means give reasons. To answer this question you should use four changes from this topic, beginning with what the attitude used to be and explaining how it has changed. Your answer should be four short paragraphs. For tips on Quality of Written Communication, look at page 3.

SUMMARY

Attitudes to the roles of men and women have changed greatly. Women now have equal rights and men and women are expected to share roles in the home. Attitudes have changed because of the Feminist Movement, social and industrial changes and the effects of the World Wars.

Topic 4.2 Different Christian attitudes to equal rights for women in religion

> *I do not permit a woman to teach or to have authority over a man; she must be silent. For Adam was formed first, then Eve. And Adam was not the one deceived; it was woman who was deceived and became a sinner.*
>
> **1 Timothy 2:12–14**

> *A wife is to submit graciously to the servant leadership of her husband even as the Church willingly submits to the leadership of Christ ... she, being in the image of God, as is her husband and thus equal to him, has the God-given responsibility to respect her husband and to serve as his helper.*
>
> **Statement by the Southern Baptist Convention of the USA, June 1998**

> *You are all sons of God through faith in Christ Jesus, for all of you who were baptised into Christ have clothed yourselves with Christ. There is neither Jew nor Greek, slave nor free, male nor female, for you are all one in Christ Jesus.*
>
> **Galatians 3:26–28**

There are different attitudes to equal rights for women in religion in Christianity:

1. The traditional attitude of Protestant Christianity

Many Evangelical Protestants teach that men and women have separate and different roles and so cannot have equal rights in religion. It is the role of women to bring up children and run a Christian home. Women should not speak in church and must submit to their husbands. It is the role of men to provide for the family and to lead the family in religion. Men must love their wives as themselves, but only men can be church leaders and teachers.

They have this attitude because:
- It is the teaching of the New Testament, which they believe is the final word of God. St Paul teaches that women should not teach or speak in church. St Paul also uses the story of Adam and Eve in Genesis to show that men have been given more rights by God because Adam was created first and it was the woman who was led astray by Satan and then led man astray.
- Although Jesus had women followers, he chose only men as his twelve apostles.
- It has been the tradition of the Church from the beginning that only men should have leadership rights in the Church.

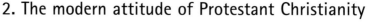

Traditional Protestant Christians believe women should grow their hair long and keep their heads covered as instructed in I Corinthians 11:3–10.

2. The modern attitude of Protestant Christianity

Many Protestant Churches now accept that men and women should have equal rights, and they have women ministers and priests (for example, Church of England, Methodist, United Reformed Church and Baptist). These Churches teach that men and women have equal rights in religion because:
- Although the story of Adam and Eve gives men priority, the creation story in Genesis 1 says that God created male and female at the same time and of equal status because both were created in the image of God.
- In some of his letters, Paul teaches that in Christ there is neither male nor female therefore men and women should have equal rights.

- There is evidence from the Gospels that Jesus treated women as his equals. He preached in the Court of Women in the Jerusalem Temple (Matthew 21:23–22:14). He treated a Samaritan woman as his equal (John 4). He had women disciples who stayed with him at the cross (Matthew 27:55, Mark 15:40–41, Luke 23:27, John 19:25–27) unlike the male disciples who ran away. It was to women that Jesus first appeared after the resurrection.
- There is some evidence that there were women priests in the early Church. The Council of Laodicea banned women priests in the fourth century and it would not have banned something that did not exist.

3. Catholic attitudes to the roles of men and women

The Catholic Church teaches that men and women should have equal roles in life and equal rights in society. Women also have all the same rights as men and are able to study and teach in theological colleges and fulfil any role in the church other than the ordained ministry (deacons, priests and bishops). They have this attitude because:

- Genesis 1:27 teaches that God created men and women at the same time and both in the image of God. So the Church teaches that men and women have equal status in the sight of God.
- It is the teaching of the Catholic Catechism that men and women are equal, and should have equal rights in life and society and Catholics should follow the teachings of the Catechism.
- In its 1971 report, 'Justice in the World', the Third World Synod of Bishops called for women to 'participate in, and share responsibility for, the life of society and of the Church'.
- Only men can be priests because the apostles were all men, and priests and bishops are successors of the apostles.
- Only men can be priests because Jesus was a man and the priest represents Jesus in the Mass.

The Lord Jesus chose men to form the college of the twelve apostles, and the apostles did the same when they chose collaborators to succeed them in their ministry ... for this reason, the ordination of women is impossible.

Catechism of the Catholic Church 1577

Should women be allowed to become bishops?

Questions

b Do you think women should have equal rights in religion? Give two reasons for your point of view. **4**

c Explain why some Christians give equal roles to women in religion and some do not. **8**

d 'Women should have equal roles in Christianity.'

  i Do you agree? Give reasons for your opinion **3**

  ii Give reasons why some people may disagree with you. **3**

Exam Tip

b You should already have thought about this, and you just have to give two reasons for your opinion. For example, if you agree with equal rights for women in religion you could use two reasons for modern Protestants agreeing with them.

SUMMARY

- Traditional Protestants believe only men should be religious leaders because this is what the Bible teaches.
- Liberal Protestants believe men and women have equal roles in religion because Jesus had women disciples.
- Catholics believe men and women should have equal roles, but only men can become priests because Jesus was a man.

Topic 4.3.1 Islam and equal rights for women in religion

There are different attitudes to equal rights for women in religion among Muslims:

1. The traditional attitude

> *Women have the same rights in relation to their husbands as are expected in all decency of them; while men stand a step above them.*
>
> **Surah 2:228**

> *Men are the ones who support women since God has given some persons advantages over others.*
>
> **Surah 4:34**

Some Muslims believe that men and women should have different roles in life and religion, and therefore they should have different rights. They believe it is the role of women to: create a halal home; have children and bring them up as good Muslims; perform their religious duties (except hajj) in the home. They believe it is the role of men to: provide for the family by working; make sure the children go to madrasah and are brought up as good Muslims; worship God in the **mosque** with their sons. They have this attitude because:

- The Qur'an teaches that men should support women because God has given men a stronger physique.
- The Qur'an teaches that women have been created to bear children, and men to provide for them.
- The Qur'an teaches that women should only inherit half of what a man inherits showing that men need more money than women to be the family providers.
- It is traditional for only men to attend the mosque and to be **imams**.

Do you think these young women in Damascus have a traditional or modern attitude?

2. The modern attitude

Some Muslims believe that men and women should have completely equal roles in religion and education. They also believe that women should have careers, but that their role as a mother should always take priority over their career. A few would accept women religious leaders. They have this attitude because:

- The Qur'an teaches that men and women are equal in religion and education.
- There is evidence from the life of the Prophet that Muhammad encouraged both men and women to worship in the mosque.
- There were women religious leaders during the early stages of Islam as seen by the fact that their advice was asked by the early **caliphs**.
- They have been affected by the non-religious arguments for equal rights for women, and see nothing in Islam that says they cannot be accepted by Muslims.

Many British Muslims mix these two attitudes and agree with women having equal rights in everything except religion.

> *Whoever works deeds of righteousness, man or woman ... verily to him will We give a new life.*
>
> **Surah 16:97**

> *The search for knowledge is a duty for every Muslim, male or female.*
>
> **Hadith quoted by al'Bukhari**

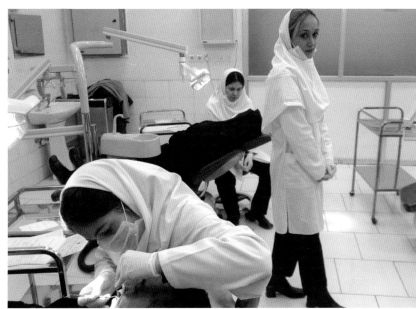

Female dentistry students at Tehran University mix modern and traditional attitudes.

Questions

b Choose one religion other than Christianity. Do you think women should have equal roles in this religion? Give two reasons for your point of view. **4**

c Choose one religion other than Christianity and explain why some followers give equal roles to women in religion and some do not. **8**

d 'Women should have the same rights as men in religion.'
  i Do you agree? Give reasons for your opinion. **3**
  ii Give reasons why some people may disagree with you. **3**

Exam Tip

d Remember to use the techniques for answering evaluation questions on page 9. Arguments for the statement would be the reasons for the modern attitude in this topic. Arguments against would be the reasons for the traditional attitude in this topic.

SUMMARY

- Traditional Muslims believe that men and women should have different roles in religion because of tradition and the teachings of the Qur'an.
- Modern Muslims believe that men and women should have equal roles in religion because of the teachings of the Qur'an and the example of the Prophet.

Topic 4.3.2 Judaism and equal rights for women in religion

There are different attitudes to equal rights for women in religion in Judaism:

1. The Orthodox attitude

Most Orthodox Jews believe that men and women have different roles and so they cannot have equal rights in religion. It is the role of women to: keep a kosher home; have children and bring them up as good Jews; fulfil most of their religious duties in the home; sit separately from the men when attending synagogue. It is the role of men to: provide for the family; make sure the children are brought up as good Jews; form a **minyan** at the synagogue; perform the ritual prayers every day; make sure the synagogue provides all the worship and education needed. Orthodox Jewish women cannot be religious leaders or rabbis.

Many Orthodox Jews give equal rights to women in life and so Orthodox women can have careers, but they do not allow equal rights in religion. They have this attitude because:

- It is the teaching of the Torah, Talmud and rabbis, which has supreme authority for most Orthodox Jews.
- The mitzvot only apply to men (the rabbis exempted women from all mitzvot applying to a particular time) therefore women cannot have the same rights in religion as men.
- The Orthodox believe these separate roles are the way for family life to develop in the way God wants.
- Women cannot form a minyan and so cannot have equal rights with men in the synagogue.
- Women cannot be witnesses in a Bet Din court and so cannot have equal rights with men in the religious laws of Judaism.

> To the woman he said, 'I will greatly increase your pain in childbearing; with pain you will give birth to children. Your desire will be for your husband and he will rule over you.
>
> **Genesis 3:16**

How can you tell this is an Orthodox synagogue?

2. The Liberal/Reform attitude

In Liberal/Reform and Progressive Judaism, men and women have completely equal rights. Women and men worship together and there are women rabbis. Women can form a minyan and be witnesses in court. They have this attitude because:

How can you tell this is not an Orthodox synagogue?

- Although the story of Adam and Eve gives men priority, the creation story in Genesis 1 says that God created male and female at the same time and of equal status therefore women should have equal rights in religion.
- They believe that the Torah is not the word of God, but is inspired by God and so can be interpreted for today. Therefore those parts of the Torah denying equal rights to women should no longer apply.
- They believe that to deny equal rights to women in religion is the same as saying that God prefers men to women and why would God prefer one part of humanity to the other?
- They believe that Judaism should relate to attitudes in the modern world and so should accept equal rights for women.

Times have changed. Women do not marry young, do not have many children. They lead their own lives as single, married or divorced women, and it is up to Reform Judaism to re-interpret the Torah in the light of these changes.

The First Jewish Catalogue

Questions

b Choose one religion other than Christianity. Do you think women should have equal roles in this religion? Give two reasons for your point of view. **4**

c Choose one religion other than Christianity and explain why some followers give equal roles to women in religion and some do not. **8**

d 'Women should have the same rights as men in religion.'
  i Do you agree? Give reasons for your opinion. **3**
  ii Give reasons why some people may disagree with you. **3**

Exam Tip

d Remember to use the techniques for answering evaluation questions on page 9. Arguments for the statement would be the reasons for the modern attitude in this topic. Arguments against would be the reasons for the traditional attitude in this topic.

SUMMARY

- Orthodox Jews believe that men and women are equal but have different roles in religion because it is the teaching of the Torah.

- Reform Jews believe that men and women have completely equal roles in religion and accept women as rabbis because God created men and women with equal status.

Topic 4.3.3 Hinduism and equal rights for women in religion

There are different attitudes to equal rights for women in religion in Hinduism:

1. The traditional attitude

Some Hindus believe that men and women have different roles and so cannot have equal rights. Men are the protectors of women and should have the role of breadwinner and leader of the household. They believe that women should look after the home and children, and care for the shrine in the home. They do not allow women to be priests or religious leaders. They have this attitude because:

- It is the teaching of the shruti scriptures, which traditional Hindus regards as divinely inspired.
- It is the teaching of the Laws of Manu, which traditional Hindus believe are the laws that must be followed to fulfil your dharma and achieve moksha.
- It is the tradition for the householder ashrama, which all Hindus must complete if they are to gain moksha.
- It is part of Indian culture, which traditional Hindus regard as part of Hinduism.

> *The father protects the woman in childhood, the husband protects her in youth, the children protect her in old age, a woman should never be independent.*
>
> **Laws of Manu**

> *Go to your husband's home and take charge of it. Occupy the main position and carry out all the activities connected with the home. Here may you have children and protect your happiness.*
>
> **Hindu Marriage service**

Why do you think some Hindus see worship in the home as a woman's role in religion?

2. The modern attitude

Some Hindus (such as **Iskcon** and the **Virashaivas**) believe that women and men should have equal rights in both life and religion. They have women religious leaders. They have this attitude because:

- They believe that all souls are actually or potentially part of the divine and so are equal. Therefore men and women should have equal rights.
- They believe that even the shruti scriptures cannot be taken literally and need interpreting in the light of modern life.

An Indian woman taking a break from cleaning the statue that commemorates the Salt March of 1930 in which both men and women marched against British rule.

- They believe that the Laws of Manu were intended for a different time and society and do not apply to modern life.
- They believe that there are other ways to gain moksha than following the traditional ashramas.

Some modern Hindus (such as the **Swaminarayan**) would say that although men and women should have equal rights in life, they should have different roles in Temple worship. So they do not give women equal rights in religion and they do not have women religious leaders.

Women from various backgrounds responded enthusiastically to Gandhi's call to participate in the national struggle for freedom (from British rule) ... It had important implications. Both men and women became equal partners in a common cause. Women were able to come out into the open and thus break the barriers of caste and sex. Women availed themselves of educational opportunities and qualified for professions such as law, medicine, teaching, social work and the like.

From *Themes and Issues in Hinduism*, edited by P. Bowen

Questions

b Choose one religion other than Christianity. Do you think women should have equal roles in this religion? Give two reasons for your point of view. **4**

c Choose one religion other than Christianity and explain why some followers give equal roles to women in religion and some do not. **8**

d 'Women should have the same rights as men in religion.'
  i Do you agree? Give reasons for your opinion. **3**
  ii Give reasons why some people may disagree with you. **3**

Exam Tip

d Remember to use the techniques for answering evaluation questions on page 9. Arguments for the statement would be the reasons for the modern attitude in this topic. Arguments against would be the reasons for the traditional attitude in this topic.

SUMMARY

- Traditional Hindus teach that men and women have different roles in religion because of the Laws of Manu.
- Modern Hindus believe that men and women should have equal roles in religion because all souls are part of the divine and so are equal.

Topic 4.3.4 Sikhism and equal rights for women in religion

There are different attitudes to equal rights for women in religion in Sikhism:

1. The religious attitude

Sikhism teaches the complete equality of men and women, and so most Sikhs believe that women should have equal rights in religion. Many gurdwara committees in Britain have women members and Sikh girls are given equal educational and career opportunities by their parents. There are some women religious leaders in Sikhism. Sikhs have this attitude because:

- **Guru Nanak** taught that gender is a creation of God, but male and female are to be seen as two halves of a whole who therefore have equal rights.
- It was the teaching of all the other Gurus. Guru Amar Das appointed women as Sikh preachers and it was a woman, Mati Sahib Kaur, the wife of Guru Gobind Singh, who mixed the **amrit** for the first **initiation ceremony** and she was admitted to the **Khalsa**.
- The Guru Granth Sahib teaches that God is neither male nor female, and so God does not give preferential treatment to either sex.
- The Guru Granth Sahib teaches that men and women have so much in common that they must be treated the same. 'Man is born of woman and woman of man.' Guru Granth Sahib 879.

> *The wise and beauteous Being is neither man nor woman nor bird.*
>
> **Guru Granth Sahib**

> *You are our mother and father, we are your children.*
>
> **Guru Granth Sahib**

Which Sikh attitude to women is shown in this **langar**?

2. The cultural attitude

Some Sikhs believe that men and women should have different roles and so cannot have equal rights in religion. They believe that men should have the role of breadwinner and leader of the household. They believe that women should look after the home and children, not be religious leaders. They have this attitude because:

- Most Sikhs come from the Punjab where women are not given equal rights with men because of the influence of traditional Hinduism and Islam.
- In Punjabi society girls are regarded as the property of their father and then their husband. This means that women cannot be given equal rights because it would lead to the breakdown of society.
- It is difficult to change cultural attitudes and some Sikhs believe that culture is part of religion.
- Most Sikhs with this attitude do not read the scriptures, nor know about the lives and teachings of the Gurus, so they do not know that Sikhs should give women equal rights.

> *From a temporal as well as spiritual point of view, woman is man's other half.*
>
> **Bhai Gurdas, a seventeenth century Sikh Scholar**

Do you think these Sikh women have a religious or cultural attitude to their role in religion?

Questions

b Choose one religion other than Christianity. Do you think women should have equal roles in this religion? Give two reasons for your point of view. **4**

c Choose one religion other than Christianity and explain why some followers give equal roles to women in religion and some do not. **8**

d 'Women should have the same rights as men in religion.'
  i Do you agree? Give reasons for your opinion. **3**
  ii Give reasons why some people may disagree with you. **3**

Exam Tip

d Remember to use the techniques for answering evaluation questions on page 9. Arguments for the statement would be the reasons for the modern attitude in this topic. Arguments against would be the reasons for the traditional attitude in this topic.

SUMMARY

- Some Sikhs believe that men and women are totally equal and should have the same roles in life and religion because this is the teaching of the Gurus.
- Some Sikhs are affected by cultural attitudes and think women should be subordinate to men and not have a role in religion.

Topic 4.4 The United Kingdom as a multi-ethnic society

KEY WORDS

Discrimination – Treating people less favourably because of their ethnicity/gender/colour/class.

Ethnic minority – a member of an ethnic group (race) which is much smaller than the majority group.

Multi-ethnic society – many different races and cultures living together in one society.

Prejudice – believing some people are inferior or superior without even knowing them.

Racism – the belief that some ethnic groups are superior to others.

The United Kingdom has always been a mixed society – Celts, Romans, Angles, Saxons, Jutes, Danes, Vikings and Normans are all ancestors of the British.

The United Kingdom has always believed in human freedom and has offered asylum to those suffering persecution; for example, to French Protestants (Huguenots) in the seventeenth century, to Russian Jews in the nineteenth century, to European Jews escaping Hitler in the twentieth century.

In the nineteenth century the United Kingdom built up an empire around the world. In exchange for being ruled by Britain, citizens of the Empire were allowed to settle in the United Kingdom. Slaves who set foot on British soil immediately became free. As a result, small black communities grew up in Bristol, Liverpool and Cardiff.

The Empire became known as the Commonwealth as nations gained their independence from the United Kingdom. In the 1950s there was substantial immigration from the Commonwealth. People came from India, Pakistan, Bangladesh, West Africa and the Caribbean to lessen a labour shortage in the United Kingdom. Many of these workers had fought for the United Kingdom in the Second World War (there were more people in the British armed forces from the Commonwealth than from the United Kingdom itself).

Traditionally, the man of the family is the provider and protector of women in Hindu families.

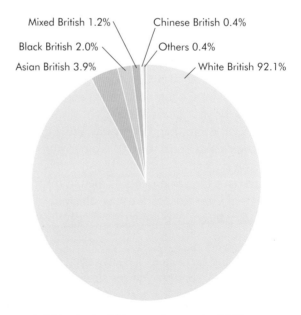

The different ethnicities in the UK, according to the 2001 census.

Source: Census 2001

Immigration from the Commonwealth has continued on a smaller scale, but the extension of the European Union at the beginning of this century led to a large influx of East Europeans, and wars and racial/religious persecutions have led to an increase of asylum seekers (people wanting to live in the UK because their lives are at risk in their own countries).

Although only 7.9 per cent of the total United Kingdom population is **ethnic minority**, there are big differences in different areas. For example 29

Why do you think the recently elected President, Barack Obama, is seen by many as a sign that the USA now truly has equal rights?

per cent of London's population is of ethnic minority origin, as opposed to less than 2 per cent of the population of South West England.

The problems of discrimination and racism

Racism is a type of **prejudice** that can cause major problems in a **multi-ethnic society** because of the **discrimination** it leads to. Racist people believe the ethnic group to which they belong to be superior to all other ethnic groups. Therefore they believe that all other races are inferior. Religiously prejudiced people believe that everyone who does not believe in their religion is wrong.

The problems of discrimination and racism:
- Racially prejudiced employers will not give jobs to certain ethnic groups, religiously prejudiced employers will not give jobs to certain religious groups (it is easy, for example, for employers to discriminate against Muslims, Sikhs and Orthodox Jews).
- Prejudiced landlords are likely to refuse accommodation to certain ethnic groups or religions.
- If teachers are prejudiced against certain ethnic minorities or religious groups, they might discriminate against them in their teaching, so that those pupils do not achieve the results (and so gain the jobs) of which they are capable. They could try to get them excluded from school, put them into lower ability groups than their actual ability, etc.
- Prejudiced police officers could potentially discriminate against certain ethnic or religious groups for example by: stopping and searching them if they had no real reason for so doing; not treating evidence from people against whom they are prejudiced in the same way that they treat evidence from people against whom they are not prejudiced.

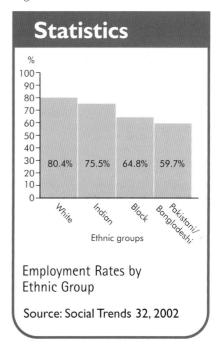

Statistics

Employment Rates by Ethnic Group

Source: Social Trends 32, 2002

Skilled immigrants from Eastern Europe, far from posing a threat, will help to raise wages in Britain and boost exports, economists predict ... Eastern European countries have plenty of skilled people with post-school education and training.

The Times, 5 April 2004

The effects of discrimination and racism

The effects of this can be quite devastating for a
multi-ethnic society:

- If certain groups feel that they are being treated unfairly by
  society, then they will begin to feel alienated by society and so
  work against that society.
- Some politicians believe that young black people turn to crime
  because they feel they will not be able to get good well-paid
  jobs because of racism and discrimination and so they might as
  well earn good money from crime. If true, this might lead to
  an increase in crime.
- Some politicians believe that some young people have been
  turning to extremist Islamic groups because they feel they have
  no chance of success in a prejudiced British society that
  discriminates against their religion. This can then lead them to
  commit terrorist acts.
- Racism and discrimination can lead to the rise of groups like
  the BNP (British National Party), which stir up hatred of
  different ethnic groups leading to violence and communal
  warfare.

A performer in the Notting Hill
Carnival in London.

If a multi-ethnic society is to function well, it must treat all its
members fairly, and give equal opportunities to all its members to
enable them to produce their best.

The benefits of living in a multi-ethnic society

Multi-ethnic societies bring far more benefits than problems:

- There is likely to be less chance of war because people of different ethnic groups and nationalities will get to know and like each other, and probably intermarry.
- More progress will be made in a multi-ethnic society because new people will bring in new ideas and new ways of doing things. Societies that are cut off and do not mix with other cultures tend to be less progressive, for example, the Amazonian Indians.
- Life is more interesting with a much greater variety of food, music, fashion and entertainment.
- A multi-ethnic society helps people to see that different ethnic groups are all part of the human race and we have more in common than we have differences. This is vital in a world of multi-national companies and economic interdependence between all nations.

How does this crowd celebrating Chinese New Year in London's Chinatown in 2007 show the UK as a multi-ethnic society?

Questions

b Do you think we need laws against racism?
Give two reasons for your point of view. **4**

c Explain why discrimination and racism cause problems in a multi-ethnic society. **8**

d 'Prejudice and discrimination should be banned.'
  i Do you agree? Give reasons for your opinion. **3**
  ii Give reasons why some people may disagree with you. **3**

Exam Tip

c 'Explain' means give reasons. To answer this question you should use four effects of discrimination and racism. Your answer should be four short paragraphs. For tips on Quality of Written Communication, look at page 3.

SUMMARY

- Britain has many ethnic minorities and so is a multi-ethnic society.
- Multi-ethnic societies have many benefits, such as advancing more quickly because they have a greater variety of ideas.
- A multi-ethnic society needs equal opportunities and treatment to work, and prejudice and discrimination cause major problems in such a society because they do not treat everyone equally.

Topic 4.5 Government action to promote community cohesion in the United Kingdom

KEY WORDS

Community cohesion –
a common vision and shared sense of belonging for all groups in society.

Multi-faith society –
many different religions living together in one society.

Nothing in this Part [of the Act] shall be read, or given effect, in a way which prohibits or restricts discussion, criticism or expressions of antipathy, dislike, ridicule, insult or abuse of particular religions ... Therefore the new offence has an even higher threshold than the race hatred offence, recognizing that religious beliefs are a legitimate subject of vigorous public debate.

Home Office Press Release 1 October 2007

Community cohesion may have prevented atrocities like the 7 July 2007 London bombings.

The United Kingdom believes that a multi-ethnic society needs to promote **community cohesion** in order to overcome the problems of prejudice, discrimination and racism. The British Government promotes community cohesion by:

- financially supporting groups that are working for community cohesion
- making community cohesion part of the national education curriculum. The Education and Inspections Act 2006 introduced a duty on all maintained schools in England to promote community cohesion and on Ofsted to report on the contributions made in this area
- funding research into the best ways of achieving community cohesion
- appointing cabinet ministers, judges, etc., from ethnic minorities
- passing the Race Relations Act, which makes it unlawful to discriminate against anyone because of race, colour, nationality, ethnic or national origins; use threatening or abusive or insulting words in public that could stir up racial hatred; publish anything likely to cause racial hatred
- passing the Crime and Disorder Act, which allows higher maximum penalties where there is evidence of racial or religious motivation or hostility
- passing the Racial and Religious Hatred Act, which makes it an offence to use threatening words or behaviour intended to incite groups of people defined by their religious beliefs or lack of belief
- establishing the Equality and Human Rights Commission, which champions equality and human rights for all
- ensuring that the Labour Party, the Conservative Party and the Liberal Democrat Party oppose racism in any form particularly by encouraging members of ethnic minorities to become MPs.

Why community cohesion is important

Community cohesion is important for all multi-ethnic and multi-faith societies because:

- Without community cohesion, different groups in society have different visions of what society should be like and this can lead to violence and civil unrest.

- A lack of community cohesion in Oldham, Burnley and Bradford led to racially/religiously motivated street rioting in 2001. According to the Government Cantle report, the rioting was caused by: different communities living 'parallel lives', ignorance about other communities being exploited by extremists and weak local leadership and policing. Single-faith schools were also criticised for raising the possibility of deeper divisions.
- The 7 July 2007 bombers on the London Underground were British citizens who had lost their sense of allegiance to Britain and, indeed, were prepared to kill, maim and injure their fellow citizens.
- In countries without community cohesion (such as Iraq, Kosovo and Kashmir) violence becomes a way of life.
- Lack of community cohesion leads to different communities leading separate lives, making civilised living impossible.

Cohesion if therefore about: how to avoid the bad efects of intolerance and harassment that can break down society; how to encourage different groups to work together and treat each other and fellow citizens; how to ensure respect for diversity whilst building up a commitment to common and shared bonds as citizens of the same society.

SUMMARY

The government is promoting community cohesion in the UK by passing laws against racism and discrimination, and by making community cohesion part of the national curriculum.

Community cohesion is important because without it a multi-ethnic society could become violent and divided.

Questions

b Do you think the government should spend money promoting community cohesion? Give two reasons for your point of view. **4**

c Explain how the government is trying to promote community cohesion. **8**

d 'Promoting community cohesion is the most important thing a government can do in a multi-ethnic society.'

   i Do you agree? Give reasons for your opinion. **3**

   ii Give reasons why some people may disagree with you. **3**

Exam Tip

c 'Explain' means give reasons. To answer this question you should use four government actions from this topic, and for each action explain how it should improve community cohesion. Your answer should be four short paragraphs. For tips on Quality of Written Communication, look at page 3.

In almost every one of the Commonwealth's 53 nations there are schools distinguished by names like King's, Queen's, Bishop's ... We studied Tudors and Stuarts. We produced **Julius Caesar, Richard II** *and* **Much Ado About Nothing** *... But there was something else we valued even more ... We believed that a liberal democratic state in which individual freedom is assured, and where talent, and hard work are rewarded, was superior to any alternative ... on offer. We were taught that, whatever your background you owed something to your country – and that all traditions could and should play a part in nation building. That we would all have, somehow, to share this space.*

... Our planet has never been more in need of that shared set of values and that common sentiment of toleration than today ... (the) Equality and Human Rights Commission has (a duty) to make sure that people who are very different can live together. It is integral to our mandate of reducing inequality, promoting human rights, strengthening good relations.

From a speech by Trevor Phillips, Head of the Equality and Human Rights Commission, January 2008

Topic 4.6 Why Christians should help to promote racial harmony

KEY WORD

Racial harmony – different ethnic groups living together peacefully.

There are many reasons why Christians should try to promote racial harmony.

1 In the Parable of the Good Samaritan (Luke 10:25–37), Jesus taught that Christians should love their neighbours and that neighbour means people of all races. Jews and Samaritans were different races who hated each other. In the parable, Jesus taught that the Good Samaritan treated the Jew who was attacked as his neighbour, so showing that Christians have to treat people of every race as their neighbour who they have to love.

'Which of these three do you think was a neighbour to the man who fell into the hands of robbers? The expert in the law replied, 'The one who had mercy on him.' Jesus told him, 'Go and do likewise.'

Luke 10:36–37

Vincent Van Gogh's painting, *The Good Samaritan*. How does the Parable of the Good Samaritan encourage Christians to promote racial harmony?

I now really understand ... that God has no favourites, but that anybody of any nationality who fears him and does what is right is acceptable to him.

Acts 10:34

2 Jesus treated a Samaritan woman as his equal (John 4); healed a Roman centurion's servant (Luke 7) and had a black African helping him to carry his cross (Luke 23:26). Christians should follow the example of Jesus and if Jesus helped promote racial harmony, so should they.

You are all sons of God through faith in Christ Jesus, for all of you who were baptised into Christ have clothed yourselves with Christ. There is neither Jew nor Greek, slave nor free, male and female, for you are all one in Christ Jesus.

Galatians 3:26–28

3 St Peter was given a vision by God (Acts 10) in which God sent down a sheet filled with all sorts of animals and told Peter to eat from them, but Peter refused because, according to Jewish law, they were unclean. A voice from heaven told him, 'What God has made clean, you have no right to call profane.' Peter believed that God was showing him that God treats all races the same and accepts the worship of anyone who does right whatever their race. St Peter was the greatest disciple and Christians should follow his example of working for racial harmony.

4 Racial harmony is taught by St Paul. As his teachings are a large part of the New Testament, which Christians claim is the word of God, his teachings should be followed by Christians. St Paul taught in Galatians 3:26–29 that everyone is equal in Christ and so there can be no divisions of race among Christians. St Paul also taught that as God created all nations from one man, Adam, all nations are therefore equal to each other.

5 The Christian Church has members from every country in the world. Almost 50 per cent of the world's population is Christian and over 70 per cent of Christians are non-white, non-European.

6 All the Christian Churches have issued statements condemning racism and encouraging all Christians to promote racial harmony. In May 1998 the Presidents of Churches Together in England published a letter condemning racism and religious hatred and asking voters and political parties involved in local elections not to be involved in any form of racism.

> *The Church rejects as foreign to the mind of Christ, any discrimination against men or harassment of them because of their race, colour, condition of life, or religion.*
>
> **Declaration on the Relationship of the Catholic Church to non-Christians**

> *Respect for the humanity we share with each and every neighbour is the only basis for a peaceful and good society. Any attack on the dignity and human rights of any racial or religious group damages all of us.*
>
> **From the Churches Together letter to the press, May 1998**

Cardinal Francis Arinze of Nigeria, suggested by some as a possible Pope, a sign of racial harmony in the Christian Church.

Questions

b Do you think Christians should help to promote racial harmony? Give two reasons for your points of view. **4**

c Explain why Christians should help to promote racial harmony. **8**

d 'If everyone were religious, there would be no racism.'
   i Do you agree? Give reasons for your opinion. **3**
   ii Give reasons why some people may disagree with you. **3**

Exam Tip

b You should already have thought about this, and you just have to give two reasons for your opinion. For example, if you agree with Christians promoting racial harmony, you could use two reasons from this topic.

SUMMARY

Christians should promote racial harmony because of the teachings of the Bible and the Church against racism, and because they should follow the example of Jesus.

Topic 4.7.1 Islam and racial harmony

The hajj is a supreme example of racial harmony in Islam. Over two million Muslims of all races and colours gather in Makkah to perform the rituals of pilgrimage as one body.

All mankind is from Adam and Eve, an Arab has no superiority over a non-Arab, nor a non-Arab has any superiority over an Arab; also a white has no superiority over a black, nor a black has any superiority over a white, except by piety and good action. Learn that every Muslim is a brother to every Muslim and that the Muslims constitute one brotherhood.

The Prophet Muhammad in his Last Sermon, 9 Dhul Hijjah 632

SUMMARY

Muslims should promote racial harmony because Islam teaches that racism is wrong because of the teachings of the Qur'an and the example of Muhammad.

There are many reasons why Muslims should try to promote racial harmony:

- The Qur'an (which is the word of God for all Muslims) teaches that all races are equal in the eyes of God. God created the whole of humanity from one pair of humans, therefore all races are related and none can be regarded as superior.
- There are many sayings of the Prophet Muhammad (hadith) that promote racial harmony. In his final sermon, Muhammad said that every Muslim is a brother to every other Muslim, and so there should be no racism among Muslims. As Muslims should follow the teachings of Muhammad, the final prophet of God, they should promote racial harmony.
- Muslims regard Muhammad as 'the great exemplar', and so they should follow his example. During his life Muhammad promoted racial harmony, for example, his first prayer caller was a black African Muslim, whereas Muhammad was an Arab, showing how Muhammad promoted racial harmony.
- Islam itself promotes racial harmony because it has members in most ethnic groups and most countries around the world. It is the world's second largest religion.
- Islam teaches that all Muslims form one brotherhood, the **Ummah**. This means that all Muslims, whatever their race, should regard each other as brothers and sisters. Forming all races into a united brotherhood is a way of promoting racial harmony.
- Islam is against any form of racism and Muslim leaders and local mosques work with various groups to promote racial harmony in the United Kingdom.

Questions

b Do you think it is important for religious people to work for racial harmony? Give two reasons for your point of view. **4**

c Choose one religion other than Christianity and explain why the followers of that religion should help to promote racial harmony. **8**

d 'Nothing does more for racial harmony than religion.'
  i Do you agree? Give reasons for your opinion. **3**
  ii Give reasons why some people may disagree with you. **3**

Exam Tip

d Remember to use the techniques for answering evaluation questions on page 9. Arguments for the statement would be the reasons for Muslims and/or Christians promoting racial harmony. Arguments against would be religious people who are racist, and groups that claim to be religious but are racist, for example, the Ku Klux Klan in the USA claimed to be Christian but used violence against black people; also the Dutch Reformed Church in South Africa taught that black people should not be treated equally.

Topic 4.7.2 Judaism and racial harmony

Although most followers of Judaism are also members of the Jewish race (though not necessarily the same ethnic group), Judaism does not regard any race as superior to another.

Judaism promotes racial harmony because:
- The Torah teaches racial harmony. It shows that all humans can be traced back to Adam and Eve and so they must all be brothers and sisters. Many rabbis interpret, 'This is the book of the generations of man' (Genesis 5:1) to mean that God did not divide people into races or colours. The main teaching of the Torah that God is one is taken by most rabbis to mean that humanity is also one because it was created by the one God.
- There is a lot of teaching in the Tenakh about how God cares for the oppressed and wants his people to bring justice to the world. This means that Jews must stop any form of racism (oppression based on race) and end the injustice of bad treatment based on race. The Tenakh teaches that Jews have been given a special responsibility by God to show God's laws to the rest of humanity and part of this responsibility must be promoting racial harmony.
- There have been many racist attacks on Jews over the past 2,000 years, culminating in the Holocaust during the Second World War when the Nazis tried to destroy the whole Jewish race. This makes it impossible for most Jews to regard racism as anything but evil.

> *Adam named his wife Eve, because she would become the mother of all the living.*
>
> **Genesis 3:20**

> *Do not abhor an Edomite, for he is your brother. Do not abhor an Egyptian, because you lived as an alien in his country.*
>
> **Deuteronomy 23:7**

> *When an alien lives with you in your land, do not ill-treat him. The alien living with you must be treated as one of your native-born.*
>
> **Leviticus 19:33–34**

An Ethiopian Jew emigrating to Israel.

Questions

b Do you think it is important for religious people to work for racial harmony? Give two reasons for your point of view. **4**

c Choose one religion other than Christianity and explain why the followers of that religion should help to promote racial harmony. **8**

d 'Nothing does more for racial harmony than religion.'
  i Do you agree? Give reasons for your opinion. **3**
  ii Give reasons why some people may disagree with you. **3**

Exam Tip

d Remember to use the techniques for answering evaluation questions on page 9. Arguments for the statement would be the reasons for Jewish people and/or Christians promoting racial harmony. Arguments against would be religious people who are racist, and groups that claim to be religious but are racist, for example, the Ku Klux Klan in the USA claimed to be Christian but used violence against black people; also the Dutch Reformed Church in South Africa taught that black people should not be treated equally.

SUMMARY

Jewish people should promote racial harmony because Judaism teaches that racism is wrong because of the teachings of the Torah and Jewish experiences in the Holocaust.

Topic 4.7.3 Hinduism and racial harmony

Many different races are members of Hare Krishna.

There are many reasons why Hindus should try to promote racial harmony:

- Hindus believe that every soul is an actual or potential part of the divine (Brahman). If every soul has the potential to be part of the divine, then every soul must be of equal value, and if every soul is of equal value, then every person (whatever their race or colour) is of equal value.

- The Indian Hindus have suffered from racist treatment when they were ruled by the Moghul, and then the British, Empires. This treatment has led Hindu leaders to work for racial harmony and justice. This was seen particularly in the work of Mohandas Gandhi who led the struggle for Indian independence based on the racial and ethnic groups in India working and living together as equals.

- Although the majority of Hindus are from India, there are many different ethnic groups in India. All these groups are treated as equal by Hindus to follow the teachings of Gandhi.

- There are also many people from ethnic groups outside India who are converting to Hinduism (groups like Iskcon are making converts in the West) who are all treated as equals by Indian Hindus.

- Hinduism is opposed to racism and racial discrimination in any form. Hindus work with many other groups in the United Kingdom to promote racial harmony.

> *When the central reality of God is all-pervasive and religion creates no barriers between man and man, then the denial of freedom and equality to all human beings is not only politically unjust, but spiritually sinful.*
>
> **The Harijan Journal**

SUMMARY

Hindus should promote racial harmony because they believe that every soul is a part of Brahman and so everyone should be treated equally.

Questions

b Do you think it is important for religious people to work for racial harmony? Give two reasons for your point of view. **4**

c Choose one religion other than Christianity and explain why the followers of that religion should help to promote racial harmony. **8**

d 'Nothing does more for racial harmony than religion.'
  i Do you agree? Give reasons for your opinion. **3**
  ii Give reasons why some people may disagree with you. **3**

Exam Tip

d Remember to use the techniques for answering evaluation questions on page 9. Arguments for the statement would be the reasons for Hindus and/or Christians promoting racial harmony. Arguments against would be religious people who are racist, and groups that claim to be religious but are racist, for example, the Ku Klux Klan in the USA claimed to be Christian but used violence against black people; also the Dutch Reformed Church in South Africa taught that black people should not be treated equally.

Topic 4.7.4 Sikhism and racial harmony

There are many reasons why Sikhs should try to promote racial harmony.

Although most followers of Sikhism are also ethnic Punjabis, Sikhism does not regard any race as superior to another. It is opposed to racism and racial discrimination in any form. Sikhs work with many other groups in the United Kingdom to promote racial harmony.

Sikhs should try to promote racial harmony because:
- The Gurus all opposed the caste system and treated people as equals whatever their race or caste.
- Guru Nanak emphasised that anyone from any background (and therefore any race) can come to salvation.
- In every Sikh act of worship **karah parshad** is shared where everyone (regardless of race or colour) eats from the same bowl, and in the langar everyone sits together to eat.
- The fundamental Sikh teaching is that because there is only one God who created the whole of humanity, humanity must also be one. Therefore there can be no differences of race or class or gender because everyone is given the divine essence.

People ignore 'untouchables' as they pass by in the streets. Why might Sikhs regard this as a form of racism?

> *Know people by the light which illumines them, not by their caste. In the hereafter, no one is regarded as different from another on grounds of caste.*
>
> **Guru Granth Sahib 349**

> *Let no one be proud of their birth. We are all born from the same clay.*
>
> **Guru Granth Sahib**

> *O, my body, God infused divine light in you and you were born into the world.*
>
> **Guru Granth Sahib 921**

Questions
b Do you think it is important for religious people to work for racial harmony? Give two reasons for your point of view. **4**
c Choose one religion other than Christianity and explain why the followers of that religion should help to promote racial harmony. **8**
d 'Nothing does more for racial harmony than religion.'
  i Do you agree? Give reasons for your opinion. **3**
  ii Give reasons why some people may disagree with you. **3**

Exam Tip
d Remember to use the techniques for answering evaluation questions on page 9. Arguments for the statement would be the reasons for Sikhs and/or Christians promoting racial harmony. Arguments against would be religious people who are racist, and groups that claim to be religious but are racist, for example, the Ku Klux Klan in the USA claimed to be Christian but used violence against black people; also the Dutch Reformed Church in South Africa taught that black people should not be treated equally.

SUMMARY
Sikhs should promote racial harmony because Sikhism teaches that racism is wrong because of the teachings of the Guru Granth Sahib and the teachings and examples of the Gurus.

Topic 4.8 The United Kingdom as a multi-faith society

Many societies were mono-faith (having only one religion) until the twentieth century. In some ways, Great Britain has been a multi-faith society ever since the Reformation in the sixteenth century. Although Queen Elizabeth I made the Church of England the state religion, there were other churches: Protestants who were not Church of England (Nonconformists), Roman Catholics and, from 1657, Jews. So Britain had to have laws encouraging religious freedom (everyone free to follow their chosen religion without discrimination). These were:

- 1688 Nonconformists were given freedom of worship.
- 1828 Nonconformists were given the same political rights as members of the Church of England.
- 1829 Roman Catholics were given the same political rights as members of the Church of England.
- 1858 Jews were given the same political rights as members of the Church of England.

These meant that members of any religion were free to worship in Great Britain and had equal political rights.

However, it was in the twentieth century that Great Britain became truly multi-faith as members of religions other than Christianity and Judaism came to Britain as immigrants (although immigrants from the Caribbean and Africa were mainly Christian).

The Census figures give the view for the whole of England and Wales, but the percentages of religions can change if you look at certain areas where some religions can be stronger:

- The London Borough of Tower Hamlets has the highest percentage of Muslims of any UK council area at 36.4 per cent.
- Leicester has the highest percentage of Hindus of any UK council area at 14.3 per cent.
- The London Borough of Barnet has the highest percentage of Jews of any UK council area at 14.8 per cent.
- Slough has the highest percentage of Sikhs of any UK council area at 9.1 per cent.
- The London Borough of Westminster has the highest percentage of Buddhists of any UK council area at 1.3 per cent.
- In Birmingham 14.4 per cent of the population are Muslim, 2.9 per cent Sikh, 2 per cent Hindu, 0.3 per cent Buddhist, 0.24 per cent Jewish.
- In Bradford 16 per cent of the population are Muslim, 1.1 per cent Sikh, 0.9 per cent Hindu.
- In the London Borough of Hounslow, there are 110,657 Christians, 16,064 Hindus, 19,378 Muslims and 18,265 Sikhs. However, many of the non-Christian religions live in the area of Southall.

Statistics

Census facts on religion in England and Wales

Christians
42,558,000 = 72.6%

No religion
8,197,221 = 14%

No answer
4,823,000 = 8.2%

Muslim
1,591,207 = 2.7%

Hindu
558,746 = 0.95%

Sikh
336,040 = 0.57%

Jewish
267,711 = 0.46%

Buddhist
149,237 = 0.25%

Other religions
157,000 = 0.27%

Source: Census 2001 ONS

The benefits of living in a multi-faith society

A multi-faith society has many benefits:

- People can learn about other religions from their friends and neighbours, and this can help them to see what religions have in common.
- People from different religions may practise their religion more seriously (for example, Muslims praying five times a day) and this may make people think about how they practise their own religion.
- People may come to understand why different religions believe what they do and this may make people think more seriously about their own religion and consider why they believe what they do.
- People are likely to become a lot more understanding about each other's religions and realise that everyone is entitled to their own opinion about religion.
- Religious toleration and understanding will exist in a multi-faith society and this may help to stop religious conflicts such as that between Protestant and Catholic Christians in Northern Ireland or between Hindus, Muslims and Sikhs in India.
- A multi-faith society may even make some people think more about religion as they come across religious ideas they have never thought about before.

Almost a quarter of the British population did not provide a specific religious preference. This alone suggests that the number of Jews is undercounted. This was not unexpected and, in fact, there are grounds for suggesting that Jews may be more reluctant than others to answer a voluntary question on religion in the census. For historical reasons, many older Jews of Central and Eastern European background are reluctant to co-operate with government-sponsored counts of Jews.

The Institute for Jewish Policy Research findings on the religious results of the 2001 census

These new religious buildings show the multi-faith nature of British society. These pictures show the Shri Swaminarayan Mandir in Neasden and the Tibetan Buddhist Temple of Samye Lings, Dumfriesshire.

SUMMARY

Britain is a multi-faith society because several religions are practised here and everyone is free to practise their religion. A multi-faith society has many benefits such as religious freedom and the opportunity to find out about, and think more deeply about, different religions.

Topic 4.9 Issues raised for religion by a multi-faith society

KEY WORDS

Interfaith marriage – marriage where the husband and wife are from different religions.

Religious pluralism – accepting all religions as having an equal right to co-exist.

Can it be right to try to convert others when living in a multi-faith society?

Tolerance is so important, and never more so for Jews and Muslims. After September 11, the imam of the local mosque came to say a prayer for peace in Arabic, and I went to the mosque to say a prayer for peace in Hebrew.

Dr J. Romaine, rabbi of Maidenhead (quoted in *The Times*, 31 March 2004)

For a multi-faith society to work, people need to have the same rights regardless of the religion they do or do not belong to (**religious pluralism**). A multi-faith society cannot accept any one religion as being the true one because that would mean that, ideally, that religion should be the only religion and so the society should be mono-faith.

Similarly a multi-faith society must have religious freedom. The people living in the society must be free to choose or reject any or all of the religions practised in the society. If all religions have equal rights, then all people must have the right to pick and choose between religions.

A society that is both religiously pluralist and has religious freedom can raise a number of issues for religion.

Conversion

Conversion is an issue because the teachings of religions and the facts of a multi-faith society conflict with each other.

1 Many religions see it as their right, and even their duty, to convert everyone to their religion because:
   * They believe that their religion is the only true religion and that all other religions are mistaken.
   * They believe that everyone should go to heaven and the only way for the followers of other religions to get to heaven is for them to be converted.
   * Their holy books teach them that they should convert non-believers.

2 Trying to convert other religions in a multi-faith society can cause major problems because:
   * Many people would say that trying to convert followers of other religions when living in a multi-faith society is a type of prejudice and discrimination. Treating people differently because of their religion and trying to convert other religions is discriminating against those who do not have the same faith as you.
   * Many people would say that it is impossible to regard all other religions as wrong unless you have studied all of them and compared them to decide which one is true. No one who is trying to convert others has done this.
   * It can lead to arguments and even violence within a multi-faith society when people are told their religion is wrong.

Bringing up children

A multi-faith society requires everyone (including children) to have religious freedom. When children reach an age where they can think for themselves about religion they must be able to choose which religion to follow, or to reject religion. It also requires that children should learn about the different religions in the society so that they can respect other religions and respect people's right to be religious or not religious as they wish. However, this causes problems for many religious believers because:

- Most religions encourage parents to ensure that their children are brought up in their religion, and become members of it; consequently many parents do not want their children to learn about other religions or have the chance to choose a different religion, or reject religion.
- Most religions teach that only those who follow their religion will have a good life after death, so religious parents are worried that they will not see their children after death unless they stay in their religion.
- Social and peer pressures compel parents to exert pressure on their children to remain in the faith to preserve family and cultural traditions.
- Children educated in state schools experience the secular nature of British life and are tempted away from religious lifestyles.

Interfaith marriages

In a multi-faith society, young people of different faiths are going to meet, fall in love and want to marry. This can raise many problems for religious parents and religious leaders because:

- Often there can be no religious wedding ceremony because both couples must be members of the same religion for a religious wedding ceremony to be allowed.
- There is a question of which religion the children of the marriage will be brought up in. Some religions insist on a child being brought up in their religion (for example, Islam and Catholic Christianity), but how can a couple decide on this?
- There is also the problem of what will happen after death? Will the couple have to be buried in separate parts of the cemetery according to their religion?
- For the parents and relatives of the couple there is often the feeling that they have betrayed their roots and family by falling in love with someone from a different religion.

Unless these issues are dealt with, then religion itself can work against community cohesion and promote conflict and hatred.

SUMMARY

A multi-faith society needs to have laws giving equal rights to all religions and to those who have no religion (religious pluralism). However, a multi-faith society can raise problems for religious people in areas such as:

- conversion attempts by other faiths because it is like discrimination
- bringing up children because they may leave their parents' faith
- interfaith marriages because of having to decide which faith the children should be brought up in.

Questions

b Do you think children should be free to choose their own religion? Give two reasons for your point of view. **4**

c Explain why mixed-faith marriages may cause problems. **8**

d 'In a multi-faith society, no religion should try to convert other people.'
  i Do you agree? Give reasons for your opinion. **3**
  ii Give reasons why some people may disagree with you. **3**

Exam Tip

b You should already have thought about this, and you just have to give two reasons for your opinion. For example, if you disagree you could use two reasons from the section on bringing up children.

Topic 4.10 Ways in which religions work to promote community cohesion in the United Kingdom

The different religions in the United Kingdom are beginning to work to promote community cohesion in the following ways.

1 Different religions are beginning to work with each other to try to discover what is the same in their religions (for example, Judaism, Islam and Christianity believe in the prophets Abraham and Moses), and from this work out ways of living together without trying to convert each other.

In September 2006, Pope Benedict XVI addressed a meeting with envoys from the Muslim world at the Pope's residence near Rome. 'I would like today to stress my total and profound respect for all Muslims,' the Pope said in the speech, adding that, 'Christians and Muslims alike must reject all forms of violence and respect religious liberty ... The inter-religious and inter-cultural dialogue between Christians and Muslims is, in effect, a vital necessity, on which a large part of our future depends.'

> *Let there be no compulsion in religion.*
>
> **Surah 2:256**

> *The lamps are different, but the light is the same.*
>
> **Rumi, a medieval Iranian Sufi, speaking about different religions**

Pope Benedict XVI meeting Muslim envoys. Do you think it is possible for Christians and Muslims to accept each other's religion?

2 Some religious groups are developing ways of helping interfaith marriages.
   - Many Protestant Churches and Liberal/Reform Jewish synagogues have developed special wedding services for mixed faith couples.
   - The Mission and Public Affairs Division of the Archbishops' Council of the Church of England has published '*Guidelines for the celebration of interfaith marriages in church*'.
   - Some religious leaders who have married partners of another religion have set up the website www.interfaithmarriage.org.uk to offer help and advice to couples from different religions.

How can you tell this is an interfaith wedding?

All nations form but one community. This is so because all stem from the one stock which God created to people the entire earth, and also because all share a common destiny, namely God ... The Catholic Church recognises in other religions that search for the God who is unknown yet near since he gives life and breath and all things and wants all men to be saved.

Catechism of the Catholic Church 842–843

All religions have a common faith in a higher reality which demands brotherhood on earth ... perhaps one day such names as Christianity, Buddhism, Islam, Hinduism will no longer be used to describe men's religious experience.

John Hick (Christian philosopher)

3 As far as issues with the upbringing of children are concerned, religions are responding in different ways:

- Some Protestant Christian Churches and Liberal/Reform Jewish synagogues encourage mixed faith parents to bring up their children in both faiths, leaving it up to the children to choose which faith to follow when they are adults.
- Leaders from the Church of England, Hindu, Sikh, Catholic, Muslim, Jewish and Buddhist faiths have signed a joint statement to follow the National Framework on Religious Education so that children in faith schools (schools following a curriculum based on one faith) will now teach the main religions practised in the United Kingdom. In their statement, the faith leaders say religious education 'enables pupils to develop respect for and sensitivity to others, in particular those whose faith and beliefs are different from their own, and promotes discernment and enables pupils to combat prejudice'.

*Religions are different roads converging to the same point. What does it matter which road we take as long as we reach the same goal?
In reality, there are as many different religions as there are individuals.*

Mohandas Gandhi

All religions should stand side by side and go hand in hand. They are one family ... like windows in an endless tapestry of man's eternal search, they give visions of Truth and Reality. And the real truth of all religion is Harmony.

His Holiness Pramukh Swami Maharaj (BAPS)

4 The main way in which religions are trying to promote community cohesion is through joining together in special groups to explore ways of helping community cohesion.

- There are national groups such as the Inter Faith Network for the UK, which was founded in 1987 to promote good relations between people of different faiths in this country. Its member organisations include representative bodies from the Baha'i, Buddhist, Christian, Hindu, Jain, Jewish, Muslim, Sikh and Zoroastrian communities; see www.interfaith.org.uk

- There are also groups in most towns and cities that bring together the different religious groups in an area to promote community cohesion between the groups, for example, Cambridge Inter-Faith Group, Concord the Leeds Interfaith Group and the Glasgow Forum of Faiths.

- There are individual places of worship that work together, for example, 'What we are trying to do in Southall is to understand other traditions by living among them and conversing with them on their terms ... Our neighbours next door are Hindus. For the last three years at Diwali, we have gone there for a meal and then gone out into the garden to set off the fireworks.' Father Michael Barnes, parish priest, St Anselm's, Southall.

The St Mungo Museum is the only museum in the UK dedicated to promoting community cohesion through religion. It is in the grounds of Glasgow Cathedral.

GLASGOW FORUM OF FAITHS DECLARATION

The current world situation has exposed the fragility of inter-faith relations and the need for an initiative that helps faith communities to listen and build relationships with each other. There is also an urgent need to show the general public that religion should not be a source of strife and that inter-faith activity is worthwhile.

The Forum of Faiths will bring together civic authorities (councillors and council officials) and the leaders of the main faith communities who have subscribed to this Declaration to work together for mutual understanding and the good of the City of Glasgow. We hope the Forum of Faiths will contribute to a better understanding of shared religious values.

The Declaration was signed by the Council leaders, the Strathclyde Police leaders and the Glasgow leaders of the Baha'i faith, the Buddhist faith, the Christian Church of Scotland (like the **URC** in England), the Christian Roman Catholic Church, the Christian Scottish Episcopal Church (like the Church of England), the Hindu faith, the Jewish faith, the Muslim faith and the Sikh faith.

To recognise the oneness of all humanity is an essential pillar of Sikhism. Some call themselves Hindus, others call themselves Muslims, but humanity worldwide is made up of one race.

Akal Ustal

This Mission is opposite the St Mungo Museum. How does it show the problems of bringing religions together?

Questions

b Do you think different religions should work together in the United Kingdom? Give two reasons for your point of view. **4**

c Explain how different religions are working together to promote community cohesion in the United Kingdom. **8**

d 'It is easy for different religions to work together in the United Kingdom.'
  i Do you agree? Give reasons for your opinion. **3**
  ii Give reasons why some people may disagree with you. **3**

Exam Tip

c 'Explain' means give reasons. To answer this question you should use the facts from this topic, but relate them very clearly to multi-faith society, explaining how the census figures in Topic 4.8 show the United Kingdom to be multi-faith, for example.

SUMMARY

Religions are working for community cohesion in the United Kingdom by:

- working to discover what is the same about religions
- helping with mixed-faith marriages
- making sure that all children learn about different faiths
- joining local and national groups to promote community cohesion.

Topic 4.11 How an issue from religion and community cohesion has been presented in one form of the media

You have to study how **one** issue from religion and community cohesion has been presented in one form of the media.

Your issue could be connected with:
- equal rights for women in religion
- problems of discrimination and racism
- equal rights for ethnic minorities
- equal rights for religious minorities
- religion and racial harmony
- issues connected with living in a multi-faith society
- religions working for community cohesion.

You have total choice of the media but it should only be one of the following:
- a soap opera
- a film
- a television drama
- a television documentary
- a radio programme
- a newspaper article in two different types of newspaper, for example, *The Times* and *The Sun*.

If you study a film such as *Bend It Like Beckham*, you must concentrate on the way it portrays Sikhs living in a multi-faith environment.

You must choose both the issue and the type of media carefully to be able to answer questions on:

- why the issue is important
- how it was presented
- whether the presentation was fair to religious beliefs
- whether the presentation was fair to religious people.

To do this you must:

1 Select an issue and a form of media. It is very important that you select only one issue. Some films have several issues running through them. If you choose more than one issue, your answers are likely to be confused.

2 Decide why the issue is important (you may need to look at the views of different members of the particular religion and of the impact of the issue on society as a whole) and why you think the producers of the media decided to focus on this issue.

Is the *Vicar of Dibley*'s presentation of equal rights for women in religion fair to religious people?

3 Write an outline of how the issue was presented, listing the main events and the way the events explored the issue.

4 Look closely at the way religious beliefs are treated in the presentation of the issue. Use this information to decide whether you think the presentation was fair to religious beliefs.

5 Look closely at the way religious people are treated in the presentation of the issue. Use this information to decide whether you think the presentation was fair to religious people.

Questions

b Do you think the media present religious people fairly? Give two reasons for your point of view. **4**

c Choose an issue from religion and community cohesion presented in one form of the media and explain whether the presentation was fair to religious people. **8**

d *You are unlikely to be asked an evaluation question on this section as you only have to study one issue in one form of the media.*

Exam Tip

c Briefly summarise the presentation, then explain why some religious people would think the presentation was fair (with reasons) and why others would think it was unfair (with reasons) then decide what you think.

SUMMARY

When studying the presentation of an issue from religion and community cohesion in the media, you must be able to explain why the issue was chosen, how it was presented, whether the presentation treated religious beliefs fairly and whether the presentation treated religious people fairly.

How to answer exam questions

Question A **What is racism?** 2 marks

The belief that some races are superior to others.

Question B **Do people from a different religion have the right to try to convert you?**

Give two reasons for your point of view. 4 marks

No I do not think they do because trying to convert followers of other religions when living in a multi-faith society is a type of prejudice and discrimination. Trying to convert other religions is discriminating against those who do not have the same faith as you.

Also trying to convert others can lead to arguments and even violence within a multi-faith society when people are told their religion is wrong.

Question C **Explain why Christians should help to promote racial harmony.** 8 marks

Christians should help to promote racial harmony because this is the teaching of Jesus, especially in the Parable of the Good Samaritan. Jesus was asked what loving your neighbour meant and he told the parable as a reply. As Samaritans and Jews hated each other and the Samaritan endangered himself to help a Jew, Jesus was clearly showing that no Christian should be racist.

Also St Peter received a vision in which God showed him that all races are equal and must be treated equally.

Finally, all the Christian Churches have made statements in favour of working for racial harmony and Christians should follow the teachings of their Church.

Question D **'Women should have the same rights as men in religion.'**

i Do you agree? Give reasons for your opinion. 3 marks

ii Give reasons why some people may disagree with you. 3 marks

i I agree with this because some Protestant Christians would agree with this because they believe that men and women were created totally equal by God. It says in Genesis 1 that God created male and female equally. Also Jesus treated women as his equals and had women disciples, showing that women should have equal rights.

ii Catholic Christians might disagree with me because they think that women cannot be priests. They believe that because Jesus only appointed men as his apostles only men can be priests. They would also argue that the priest represents Jesus at Mass and as Jesus was a man, only male priests can celebrate Mass.

QUESTION A
A high mark answer because it gives a correct definition.

QUESTION B
A high mark answer because an opinion is backed up by two developed reasons.

QUESTION C
A high mark answer because a developed reason for promoting racial harmony (the Good Samaritan) is backed up by two other reasons. A formal style of English is used and there is good use of specialist vocabulary – parable, Jesus, Jews, Samaritans, St Peter, vision, Christian Churches.

QUESTION D
A high mark answer because it states the candidate's own opinion and backs it up with three clear reasons for thinking that women should have the same rights as men. It then gives two reasons with one developed for Catholics disagreeing and believing that only men can be priests.

Glossary

Key words

Abortion the removal of a foetus from the womb before it can survive

Adultery a sexual act between a married person and someone other than their marriage partner

Agnosticism not being sure whether God exists

Assisted suicide providing a seriously ill person with the means to commit suicide

Atheism believing that God does not exist

Civil partnership a legal ceremony giving a homosexual couple the same legal rights as a husband and wife

Cohabitation living together without being married

Community cohesion a common vision and shared sense of belonging for all groups in society

Contraception intentionally preventing pregnancy from occurring

Conversion when your life is changed by giving yourself to God

Discrimination treating people less favourably because of their ethnicity/gender/colour/class

Ethnic minority a member of an ethnic group (race) which is much smaller than the majority group

Euthanasia the painless killing of someone dying from a painful disease

Faithfulness staying with your marriage partner and having sex only with them

Free will the idea that human beings are free to make their own choices

Homosexuality sexual attraction to the same sex

Immortality of the soul the idea that the soul lives on after the death of the body

Interfaith marriage marriage where the husband and wife are from different religions

Miracle something which seems to break a law of science and makes you think only God could have done it

Moral evil actions done by humans which cause suffering

Multi-ethnic society many different races and cultures living together in one society

Multi-faith society many different religions living together in one society

Natural evil things which cause suffering but have nothing to do with humans

Near-death experience when someone about to die has an out of body experience

Non-voluntary euthanasia ending someone's life painlessly when they are unable to ask, but you have good reason for thinking they would want you to do so

Nuclear family mother, father and children living as a unit

Numinous the feeling of the presence of something greater than you

Omni-benevolent the belief that God is all-good

Omnipotent the belief that God is all-powerful

Omniscient the belief that God knows everything that has happened and everything that is going to happen

Paranormal unexplained things which are thought to have spiritual causes, for example, ghosts, mediums

Prayer an attempt to contact God, usually through words

Prejudice believing some people are inferior or superior without even knowing them

Pre-marital sex sex before marriage

Procreation making a new life

Promiscuity having sex with a number of partners without commitment

Quality of life the idea that life must have some benefits for it to be worth living

Racial harmony different ethnic groups living together peacefully

Racism the belief that some ethnic groups are superior to others

Re-constituted family where two sets of children (step-brothers and step-sisters) become one family when their divorced parents marry each other

Reincarnation the belief that, after death, souls are reborn in a new body

Religious experience an experience that makes the person having the experience feel the presence of God

Religious freedom the right to practise your religion and change your religion

Religious pluralism accepting all religions as having an equal right to co-exist

Re-marriage marrying again after being divorced from a previous marriage

Resurrection the belief that, after death, the body stays in the grave until the end of the world, when it is raised

Sanctity of life the belief that life is holy and belongs to God

Sexism discriminating against people because of their gender (being male or female)

Voluntary euthanasia ending life painlessly when someone in great pain asks for death

Christian terms

Apostles' Creed a short statement of what Christians believe

Baptism sacrament of initiation using water to symbolise the cleansing of sin

Baptist a member of the Baptist Church (a Protestant Church that practises believers' baptism)

Born again the belief of some Christians that acceptance of Jesus as a personal saviour brings forgiveness of sins and a second birth in Christ

Catechism a long statement of all the beliefs of the Catholic Church

Catholic member of the Christian Church led by the Pope (Bishop of Rome)

Church of England the national Church led by the Archbishop of Canterbury and the Queen

Confirmation sacrament in which a person confirms the vows made on their behalf at their baptism

Consecrate to make holy (used to describe what the priest does to the bread and wine in the Eucharist)

Covenant an agreement

Creationism the belief that God created the universe in the way described in the Bible

Creed a summary of Christian beliefs

Dedication special service for the babies of Christians who believe in believers' baptism

Eucharist the thanksgiving service using bread and wine (also called Holy Communion)

Evangelical Protestants Protestants who regard the Bible as the absolute word of God and the only authority for Christians

Gospel literally Good News, used for accounts of the life of Jesus (written by Matthew, Mark, Luke, John)

John the Divine the author of the last book in the Bible (Revelation)

Just war the religious idea that a war can be right in certain circumstances

Liturgy service with a set ritual, e.g. the Eucharist

Mass Catholic service that includes the Eucharist

Methodist member of the Protestant Church that broke from the Church of England in the eighteenth century under John Wesley

Minister a specially chosen (ordained) leader in Churches that do not have priests (e.g. the Methodist Church)

Moses Jewish leader who was given the Ten Commandments

New Testament 27 books forming the second part of the Christian Bible

Orthodox a member of the Eastern Churches led by Patriarchs that share the faith based on Constantinople

Pentecostal Protestant Churches that emphasise the gifts of the Holy Spirit

Protestant Churches separated from the Catholic and Orthodox Churches by the emphasis on the Bible as the authority for Christians

Roman Catholic see **Catholic**

Sacrament an outward sign of an inward blessing such as baptism and the Eucharist

Salvation being freed from the power of sin and made ready for eternal life

Salvation Army Christian group founded by William Booth to bring Christianity to the working classes of Britain

Secular something that is not religious

Sin an act against the will of God

St Paul leader of the Early Church who wrote many of the letters in the New Testament

Ten Commandments rules for living given by God to Moses

URC the United Reformed Church, a Protestant Church

Hindu terms

Ahimsa non-violence, respect for life

Arti welcoming ceremony in worship

Ashrama a stage of life

Atman the self or soul

Avatar in Hindu philosophy this means the 'descent' or incarnation of a divine being (deva) or the Supreme Being (God) onto planet Earth

Bhagavad Gita the Song of Krishna, one of the most important Hindu scriptures

Brahman the ultimate reality

Caste the idea that people are born into a particular part of society according to their deeds in their last life

Dharma religious duty

Guru a spiritual teacher

Iskcon the International Society for Krishna Consciousness (a Hindu group sometimes known as Hare Krishnas)

Karma actions or deeds, often called the law of cause and effect

Krishna an avatar (descent to earth) of the God Vishnu

Law of Karma the belief that every action has an effect on the state of the soul and the chances of gaining moksha

Laws of Manu an ancient scripture of instructions on how Hindus should live

Mandir a temple

Moksha liberation from the cycle of rebirth

Nirvana the state after moksha about which Hindus have differing ideas

Puja worship

Samsara the eternal cycle of birth, death and rebirth

Shikshapatri of Lord Swaminarayan the book of the teachings of Lord Swaminarayan, founder of the Swaminarayan group (BAPS)

Shiva one of the principal deities of Hinduism

Shrine a focus of worship usually with statues of gods/goddesses

Swami a religious teacher

Swaminarayan a Hindu group also known as BAPS (Worldwide Bochasanwasi Shri Akshar Purushottam Swaminarayan Sanstha)

Upanishads Hindu scriptures that explain the Vedas

Vedas the first Hindu scriptures

Virashaivas a Hindu group following Vishnu

Jewish terms

Bet Din a Jewish court of law

Brit milah circumcision

Chuppah canopy used for the wedding ceremony

Get a certificate of divorce

Halakhah the Jewish way of life set out in the mitzvot

Kosher foods permitted for Jews

Liberal Jews a group of Progressive Jews who are more liberal than the Reform Jews

Minyan the number of men over bar mitzvah age required for an Orthodox synagogue (usually 10)

Mitzvot the laws of the Torah

Orthodox Jews those Jews who follow the Torah and halakhah literally

Progressive Jews a term used to describe both Liberal and Reform Jews

Rabbi an ordained Jewish teacher/religious leader

Reform Jews those Jews who think the Torah needs interpreting in the light of the modern world

Shabbat the seventh day, day of rest (sunset Friday to sunset Saturday)

Shema the verse from Deuteronomy which states God's oneness and is used by Jews in the mezuzah, etc to remind themselves of God's unity

Synagogue building for prayer, worship, education, social activities

Talmud collection of commentaries on the Torah

Ten Commandments rules for living given by God to Moses

Tenakh the Jewish Bible

The Temple the original centre of Judaism in Jerusalem destroyed in 70CE

Thirteen Principles of Faith a summary of Jewish beliefs, written by Maimonides

Torah the five books of Moses containing the Law

Yom Kippur the most solemn and important of the Jewish holidays

Muslim terms

Aqiqa the birth ceremony for Muslim children

Arafat a plain near Makkah where pilgrims confess their sins when on Hajj

Caliph leader of the Islamic community

Coitus interruptus generally refers to any extraction of the penis prior to ejaculation during intercourse

Five Pillars the basis of Islam: Shahadah, Salah, Zakah, Sawm (Ramadan), Hajj

Hadith sayings of the Prophet Muhammad

Hajj the annual pilgrimage to Makkah, which is the fifth pillar

Halal food permissable according to Islamic Law

Iddah the waiting period between asking for a divorce and the divorce being finalised

Imam prayer leader/community leader

Madrasah evening/weekend school attached to a mosque

Mahr the amount of money agreed to be paid by the groom and held in trust for the bride

Makkah city where Muhammad was born and where the Ka'bah is located

Mosque Muslim place of worship more correctly called a masjid

Prophet Muhammad the final prophet of Islam

Qur'an the holy book of Islam

Ramadan the ninth month of the Islamic year when all Muslims should fast (Sawm)

Salah the five daily prayers, which are the second pillar

Shahadah the declaration of Muslim faith, which is the first pillar

Shari'ah the holy law of Islam

Shirk the sin of associating things with Allah

Surah a division of the Qur'an; there are 114 surahs

Ummah the worldwide Muslim community

Zakah a tax Muslims must pay for the poor, which is the third pillar

Sikh terms

Amrit sanctified liquid made of sugar and water

Caste system the system that gave a position in society based on performance in previous lives

Gurdwara Sikh place of worship

Gurmukh God-centred, one who lives by the Guru's teaching

Guru Amar Das the third Sikh Guru

Guru Gobind Singh the tenth Guru and founder of the khalsa

Guru Granth Sahib the Sikh holy book

Guru Nanak the first Guru and founder of Sikhism

Initiation ceremony a ceremony to mark a person joining a religion

Karah parshad sanctified food shared in Sikh worship

Karma actions or deeds, often called the law of cause and effect

Khalsa the community of initiated Sikhs

Langar the gurdwara dining hall and the food served in it

Lavan the wedding hymn

Law of Karma the belief that every action has an effect on the state of the soul and the chances of gaining moksha

Manmukh self-centred, human-centred (opposite of gurmukh)

Mukti liberation from the cycle of birth, death, rebirth

Rahit Maryada the Sikh code of discipline (regulations on how to live as a Sikh)

Samsara the eternal cycle of birth, death and rebirth

Ten Gurus the ten human Gurus beginning with Guru Nanak and ending with Guru Gobind Singh

Index

The Publishers would like to thank the following for permission to reproduce copyright material:

Photo credits

p.1 © Peter Barritt/Alamy; **p.2** © Hodder Education; **p.4** © Lucien Aigner/Corbis; **p.5** © akg-images; **p.6** © Polak Matthew/Corbis Sygma; **p.7** © Reuters/Corbis; **p.8** © Reuters/Corbis; **p.11** © *t* Corbis, *b* Jill Watton; **p.12** © Royal Observatory, Edinburgh/aatb/Science Photo Library; **p13** © Kevin Schafer/Corbis; **p.14** © Private Collection/The Stapleton Collection/The Bridgeman Art Library; **p.16** © Deep Light Productions/Science Photo Library; **p.17** © Wesley Hitt/Alamy; **p.19** Punit Paranjpe/Reuters/Corbis; **p.20** © Peter Turnley/Corbis; **p.21** © STRDEL/AFP/Getty Images; **p.22** © Caritas Makeni/CAFOD; **p.23** © Bubbles Photolibrary/Alamy; **p.24** © Tigeraspect productions; **p.25** © Martin Jenkinson/Alamy; **p.26** © imagebroker/Alamy; **p.27** © Tigeraspect productions; **p.29** *l* © Stockfolio/ Alamy, *r* © Jill Watton **p.31** *t* © Digital Art/Corbis, *b* © The London Art Archive/Alamy; **p.33** © Jill Watton; **p.34** © World Religions Photo Library; **p.35** © Reuters/Corbis; **p.37** © World Religions Photo Library; **p.38** © Christie's Images Ltd.; **p.39** © Bojan Brecelj/Corbis; **p.40** © World Religions Photo Library; **p.41** © World Religions Photo Library; **p.43** *l* © Action Press/Rex Features, *r* © Action Press/Rex Features; **p. 44** © United Press International, Inc; **p.45** © Henry Westheim Photography/Alamy; **p.46** © Janine Wiedel/Photofusion; **p.47** © Steve Bell/Rex Features; **p.48** © Clouds Hill Imaging Ltd./CORBIS **p.49** © Corbis; **p.51** © Robert Fishman ecomedia/dpa/Corbis; **p.52** © Robert Nickelsberg/Liaison/Getty Images; **p.53** © Dr Najeeb Layyous/Science Photo Library; **p.55** © AAP Image/Dave Hunt; **p.57** © John Cole/Science Photo Library; **p.58** © Bibliotheque Nationale, Paris, France/The Bridgeman Art Library; **p.59** © Liba Taylor/Corbis; **p.60** © Angelo Hornak/Corbis; **p.63** © Akhtar Soomro/epa/Corbis; **p.64** © Shahaf Twizer/epa/Corbis; **p.65** © David Levenson/Getty Images; **p.67** © Victor Watton; **p.68** © Photofrenetic/Alamy; **p. 69** © Corbis; **p.70** © Daniel Hambury/EPA/Corbis; **p.72** © RubberBall/Alamy; **p.73** © Israel images/Alamy; **p.74** © Charles & Josette Lenars/Corbis; **p.75** © Circa Religion Photo Library/Twin Studio; **p.76** © Norbert Schaefer/Corbis; **p.77** © Images.com/Corbis; **p.79** © John R. Rifkin; **p.81** © Charles Bowman/photolibrary.com; **p.83** © World Religions Photo Library; **p.84** © Fiona Hanson/PA Photos; **p.85** © World Religions Photo Library; **p.86** © David Grossman/Alamy; **p.87** © Bruno Vincent/Getty Images; **p.88** © Jim Bourg/Reuters/Corbis; **p.89** © C. Lyttle/zefa/Corbis; **p.91** © David Levenson/Getty Images; **p.92** © Rob Elliott/AFP/Getty Images; **p.94** © Bettmann/Corbis; **p.96** © Monkey Business Images Ltd/photolibrary.com; **p.98** © Emma Wood/Alamy; **p.99** © Jennifer Leigh Sauer/Photonica/Getty Images; **p.101** © PA Wire/PA Photos; **p.102** © Ted Horowitz/Corbis; **p.103** © Fox Photos/Getty Images; **p.104** © Eduardo Verdugo/AP/PA Photos; **p.105** © Peter Southwick/AP/PA Photos; **p.106** © Lynsey Addario/Corbis; **p.107** © Kaveh Kazemi/Getty Images; **p.108** © Nathan Benn/Alamy; **p.109** © Motte JulesABACA/PA Photos; **p.110** © ASIM TANVEER/Reuters/Corbis; **p.111** © Jewel Samad/AFP/Getty Images; **p.112** © World Religions Photo Library; **p.113** 20th Century Fox/Everett/Rex Features; **p.114** © World Religions Photo Library; **p.115** © Larry W. Smith/epa/Corbis; **p.116** © Reuters/Corbis; **p.117** © Robert Read/Alamy; **p.118** © Peter Macdiarmid/epa/Corbis; **p.120** Todd Gipstein/Corbis; **p.121** © Grzegorz Galazka/Corbis; **p.122** © World Religions Photo Library; **p.123** © David H. Wells/Corbis; **p.124** © Tim Hawkins; Eye Ubiquitous/Corbis; **p.125** © Behzad Bernous/Zuma/Corbis; **p.127** *l* and *r* © CIRCA Religion Photo Library; **p.128** © Bob Battersby/BDI Images; **p.130** © AP Photo/PA Photos; **p.131** © Michael J. Doolittle/The Image Works; **p.132** *l* and *r* © Jill Watton; **p.133** © Jill Watton; **p.134** © 20th Century Fox/Everett/Rex Features; **p.135** © Courtesy of Dawn French.

Acknowledgements

Keith Augustine: 'The Case Against Immortality' from *www.infidels.org*, reprinted by permission of the author; Catholic Truth Society: Cardinal Hume, 'A Note on the teaching of the Catholic Church concerning Homosexual People' (1995), courtesy of the Catholic Truth Society, London; Church Times: Statement from *Report on Faith and Homophobia* (2007); Continuum International Publishing Group: Catechisms from *The Catechism of the Catholic Church* (Continuum, 2002); Edexcel: Examination questions; Equality and Human Rights Commission: Trevor Phillips, speech on religious toleration (January 2008), reprinted by permission of the Equality and Human Rights Commission; Glasgow City Council: Declaration from *Glasgow Forum of Faiths* (Glasgow City Council, 2005), reprinted by permission of Glasgow City Council and Glasgow Forum of Faiths; Islamic Propagation Centre International: quotes from *The Holy Qur'an: English Translation, Commentary and Notes with Full Arabic Text*, translated by Abdullah Ali Usuf (IPCI, 2001); John Murray Publishers: John Betjeman, lines from 'In Westminster Abbey' from *John Betjeman's Collected Poems* (John Murray, 1972), reprinted by permission of the publisher; quotes from *Holy Bible: New International Version* (Hodder & Stoughton, 1999), reprinted by permission of the publisher; News International Syndication: quote from *The Times* (7 September, 2002), © News International Syndication 2002, reprinted by permission of the publisher; Office for National Statistics: Table - Number of abortions carried out in England and Wales, 1971–2006, © Crown copyright; Pearson Education: Piara Singh Sambhi: quotes from *Guru Granth Sahib (Discovering Sacred Texts)* (Heinemann Library, 1994), reprinted by permission of the publisher; Penguin Books Ltd: Juan Mascaro (translator), quotes from *The Bhagavad Gita* (Penguin Classics,1970).

Every effort has been made to establish copyright and contact copyright holders prior to publication. If contacted, the publisher will be pleased to rectify any omissions or errors at the earliest opportunity.